Making American Folk Art Dolls

THE HOBBY INDUSTRY OF AMERICA
PROMOTES ACHIEVEMENT

Making American Folk Art Dolls

Gini Rogowski
and
Gene DeWeese

Chilton Book Company
Radnor, Pennsylvania

Photographs by ROBERT WAY
Drawings by PAUL SINTAK

Library of Congress Cataloging in Publication Data

Rogowski, Gini, 1931–
    Making American folk art dolls.

    (Chilton's creative crafts series)
    Includes index.
    1. Dollmaking. 2. Folk art—United States.
I. DeWeese, Gene, joint author. II. Title.
TT175.R64   1975   745.59'22   75-24965
ISBN 0-8019-6122-X
ISBN 0-8019-6123-8 pbk.

For the memory of my father
FRANK HANNEMAN

Contents

List
of
Illustrations

List of Color Illustrations

Introduction

Folk art, according to the definition, is simply "art of the folk"—that is to say, you and me and several million other people.

If there is one field in which that definition holds true, it's the field of folk art dolls. Anybody and everybody can get into the act. Not long ago, for instance, my eight-year-old presented me with a doll she had made from a Q-tip®, a pipe cleaner and a bit of Kleenex®. It wasn't particularly beautiful and it took a little imagination to see what it was supposed to be, but it also took some imagination to think of it in the first place. And as far as I'm concerned, that's what folk art—particularly folk art dolls—is all about: imagination.

A quick look at a few of the materials that have been used and are still being used in making these dolls will show you what I mean. There are, for example, dolls made of all kinds of dried fruits—apples, pears, apricots, even prunes. Nuts, too, come in for a lot of use, especially the everpresent acorn. Then there are pipe cleaners, wishbones, clay, birchbark, grass, corn husks and stalks, driftwood, leather, gourds, corks, you name it. I've seen or made dolls using all of these materials and more. I once even saw one made from a duck's bill, although I have to admit that one didn't appeal to me very much.

This book, of course, is not meant to be comprehensive. In a field such as this, where the accent is on individual imagination and creation, a book covering everything would be impossible. This book, then, is primarily an introduction and a sampler. It tells you how to get started, how to work with such raw materials as apples and papier mâché and how to make at least one specific doll of each type. After that, however, you're on your own. With the raw materials information and the practice you get from making the specific dolls, you should be able to go on to make just about any type of doll you want. You'll most likely be surprised and delighted at where your imagination will lead you if you give it half a chance.

As to why anyone would ever want to make dolls, particularly the weird kind I often find myself putting together, I can only speak for myself and say that it has always been great fun, whether I've been copying a traditional doll or experimenting haphazardly with a creation of my own.

I got started quite accidentally several years ago when a neighbor gave me an ancient, disintegrating doll that had belonged to her grandmother. Even now I'm not sure why, unless the poor battered thing aroused my maternal instinct, but I decided to fix it up.

That was the beginning and from there on it was all downhill on an icy street. One doll led to another and repairing dolls led to making them; making led to collecting and soon I was up to my neck in dolls of all kinds. I've been that way ever since, even though I've been giving most of the repaired dolls —the ones that can be played with, at least—to a local school for retarded children. At the moment I have several hundred dolls that I've either purposely collected or just couldn't bear to part with after I'd repaired or made them.

Then there's a filing cabinet full of patterns and articles, plus folders full of photos. And, to be cut up and used in future projects, there are two wardrobe trunks full of discarded and/or worn out clothes. Not to mention a dresser full of odds and ends that, if the proper inspiration ever strikes, will no doubt be just what I need. Altogether, this unlikely accumulation takes up nearly two full rooms. There's nothing that says you have to go to these extremes, however. In fact, you're better off if you don't: believe me, I speak from experience.

A more practical approach, particularly for those readers who might like to combine a little profit with their fun, is to sell at least some of the dolls you make. Though I have so far limited myself to selling a few each year to pick up some extra Christmas and birthday money, I know from the stories of other dollmakers and from the offers I've gotten from local gift and tourist shops that there is a good market for them. Quaint or unique things seem always to be in demand. The last chapter in this book gives you information on selling dolls at craft exhibits or on consignment, as well as a couple of pointers on displaying the dolls for sale or for your own enjoyment at home.

As for myself, it has always been the enjoyment and the variety that kept me going and I hope some of that enthusiasm shows through in this book. If you have half as much fun as I've had these last few years, about all I can say is, welcome to the club.

And If you come up with any really wild looking new dolls, drop me a line . . .

Making
American
Folk
Art
Dolls

Chapter 1

Equipment and Raw Materials

Before you can make very many dolls, you'll need some equipment to work with. You won't need very much, however, and you may already have much of it lying around the house. Even if you don't, it isn't particularly expensive and all the really essential items can be picked up at variety or department stores for a few dollars. The raw materials out of which individual types of dolls are made are covered in specific chapters, but I'll discuss several clothing materials later in this chapter.

Tools and Equipment

All the tools and equipment you'll need to make any of the dolls in this book are listed below. I've included a few comments about most of them, partly to give you an idea of what they're used for, but mostly to let you know what to look for and what to watch out for when buying them. I've also included a few items that, while not strictly necessary, are handy to have around.

Two Pair of Scissors. One pair, of average size, is to cut the fabric for most of the patterns. A smaller pair, either embroidery or manicure scissors, is to cut and trim especially small pieces of fabric.

Sewing Needles. The assortment you get on a 20- or 30-cent card at any variety store will be more than enough.

Large-Eyed Embroidery Needles. The assortment you get in a package at a variety store is sufficient. Just be sure that at least one needle has an eye large enough to take either yarn or the heavy string used to attach arms and legs to stuffed felt dolls (Chapter 17).

Thimble. A necessity if you're going to do much sewing by hand. It not only makes it easier to push the needle through the fabric, but it also keeps your needle-pushing finger from getting punctured by the wrong end of the needle. (Which means it also keeps you from getting those annoying little spots of blood on your almost-finished work.) A thimble should fit snugly enough to keep it from falling off but not so tightly that, when you pry it off, your finger has turned white.

Needlenose Pliers. These are mostly for working with the wire when you're making wire and pipe cleaner bodies. Unless you make very large bodies, anything heavier than needlenose pliers are too clumsy to use easily.

Wire Cutters. Before getting these, check your pliers. Most needlenose pliers have wire cutters built in, in which case you don't need separate cutters. Whatever you do, *don't* use scissors to cut even the flimsiest wire. In the first place, cutting wire with scissors is hard to do, and in the second, wire tends to wreck scissors beyond repair very rapidly.

Dowel Rod. A piece of ¼″ dowel rod a few inches long is handy for stuffing things. Any blunt rod will do. A brand new, unsharpened pencil, for example, works very well. *Never* use the eraser end of a sharpened pencil. It's much too easy to slip and damage yourself, especially since you have to poke pretty hard to stuff some of the items properly.

Felt Marking Pens. Fine-tipped marking pens are handy. Red and black are the most useful for painting features on any of the heads, such as those made of nuts, corks or corn husks.

Tape Measure. Actually, while this is handy, most of the things you will make will be small enough for a ruler to work just as well.

Tweezers or Forceps. Either of these is primarily to help turn the sewn-up garments inside out. The forceps, because their jaws lock in place, are very handy for holding things; they're almost like a third hand. Forceps can be ordered from most doll supply houses for a dollar or two. Medical supply houses and some drug stores also carry them.

Leather Punch. This would be used only in making shoes and in making the rawhide baby in Chapter 15, if you get some tough leather. In either case, you could probably get along without it and simply force the needle through. It may be a bit hard, but it can be done.

Thread. Mostly you will need an assortment to match the fabrics you use. A spool of strong carpet thread often comes in handy, too; you will need some strong string or twine for a few special items such as the felt dolls.

White Glue. You will need a quantity of any nontoxic, water soluble white glue that becomes clear as it dries, such as Elmer's®.

Paints. A word of warning is in order here. For dolls that are purely for display, you can get small containers of hobby or model paints in the craft or hobby sections of most variety stores. These give a very hard surface and an excellent shine, but they are both toxic and flammable, so they are certainly not suitable for anything that would be given to small children. Personally, I prefer to use *acrylics:* while they don't give the shine or hardness of the model paints and enamels, *they are nontoxic and nonflammable.* Of almost equal importance, acrylics can be washed off the brushes—and your hands—with soap and water. If you can't find acrylics in small enough quantities in a variety or hardware store, you may have to go to an artist supply shop, a hobby or craft shop, or a stationery store.

Brushes. The small artist's brushes you can get for a few cents each at most variety stores work quite well for painting faces, hair, etc.

Lipsticks and Cotton Swabs. These come in handy to give certain dolls rosy cheeks. Rather than buying full-sized lipsticks for this limited use, I generally save those tiny samples that cosmetics salesmen give away. One thing you can't use the lipstick on, though, is a vinyl doll. I'm not sure why, but the color is impossible to remove, ever. At least I've never found a way of getting it out. On most other dolls, particularly organic ones such as wood or corn husk, it works very well and can be easily wiped off if you don't do it right the first time.

Clear Shellac or Nail Polish. These are used for coating and preserving. If you have shellac on hand, fine, but if you don't, you needn't rush out and buy a can. It comes in quantities far too large for our purposes. More practical is a small bottle of clear nail polish. The smallest bottle you can get is more than enough to get you started.

Pencil, Paper and Graph Paper. Mostly you will use this for tracing patterns or making your own pattern. To enlarge the patterns in this book to full size, you'll need graph paper with two-inch squares.

X-acto® Knife. This is a small, extremely sharp hobby knife for which you can get several interchangeable blades. For someone who tends to be a bit clumsy (like me), a reasonably sharp paring knife or jackknife works about as well and a lot more safely. You might find the X-acto useful for making the carved-head dolls in Chapter 11, particularly those made of balsa wood.

Hobby Drill. This is nice to have, but it's far from being a necessity. Most things you use it for can, with a little extra work, be accomplished using anything with a sharp point, such as an ice pick. It would be used primarily for drilling holes in some of the nuts you use for heads in Chapter 7.

A Sewing Machine. Like the hobby drill, this is nice to have but it's not an absolute necessity, though it's closer to being one than is the drill. The stitching you use to make certain of the yarn wigs, for instance, could turn into an all-day job if you did it by hand. On the other hand, nothing says you ever have to make those particular types of wigs.

These, then, are all the pieces of equipment you will need to make any of the dolls in this book, not to mention the dozens of other dolls you will no doubt soon be improvising yourself.

Raw Materials

Since the materials required for specific dolls are discussed in detail in the individual chapters on those dolls, there's no point in listing them here. A few general comments applicable to most of the dolls, however, might be helpful.

FABRICS

First, there is the cloth. Since most of the dolls have to be dressed in one way or another, you will probably use more cloth than you will any other single item. I always try to get good quality, closely woven cotton materials, particularly for dolls that are meant to be played with rather than displayed. It takes a fairly sturdy material to stand up to a lot of playing and a lot of washing. The types I like best are *denim, percale,* and *unbleached muslin.*

The fact that you want good quality material, however, does not mean that you have to pay premium prices for it. In fact, you may not have to pay for it at all. If your family is anything like mine, there are any number of discarded shirts, dresses, trousers, etc., that you just haven't managed to throw away yet. Before you throw them away, simply cut out and save pieces of fabric from unworn sections.

If discarded clothes don't provide you with enough variety, try the remnant tables in any sewing shop. Remnants are usually only half price, and they are more than big enough for doll clothes. Look for remnants of ribbons, braid and embroidered trimming, too. They're usually too small for anything but dolls and they can sometimes be had for the asking. Even if they're not free, you can probably find small bags of assorted rickrack and ribbon for very reasonable prices.

Rummage sales, too, are good places to look for pieces of leftover fabric. Watch for old hats, too. When cut into very small pieces, they can make excellent trimming and decoration.

Another fabric you will need, though in lesser quantities, is *felt*. Here again you should look for good quality material and it, too, can be found in fairly inexpensive remnants. The best way to check the quality of felt is simply to hold it up to the light. If the light doesn't show through, the felt is probably good. The kind you get at some discount stores is often so flimsy that, when you try to stuff a body made of it, the seams pull out. It may even tear in some of the thin spots.

As for specific colors of cloth, that will be largely left up to you. Specific colors for specific costumes are sometimes recommended, but the materials list in each chapter generally specifies nothing more restrictive than, for example, "a colorful print" or "a pastel." Keep an eye out for small pieces of particularly bright or contrasting colors, though. They make excellent accessories—purses, bow ties and that sort of thing.

ACCESSORIES

For materials other than cloth, I can only say do your best but don't worry if you can't find the precise items called for. In the beginning, of course, while you're still learning, it's a good idea to stick as closely as you can to the listed items, but even so, don't feel overly restricted. If you don't have the exact material or if something else occurs to you, try it. Experiment. If it doesn't work, you can always try again. As with most homemade things, half the fun can be in finding something that works just as well or maybe even better. If the substitute works really well, you can always tell your friends that you planned it that way all along. It was just your own individual interpretation. This, incidentally, is one of the basic tenets of most folk art: make a virtue out of necessity whenever possible.

As time goes by and you make more and more dolls, you will find that it's a good idea to have a collection of odds and ends on hand. Try not to get carried away, though. If you're a packrat at heart, you will soon start thinking that someday you will be able to find a use for almost anything, no matter how useless it may seem at the moment. Before you know it, you will have reached the point where you hate to throw *anything* away; you just know that one of these days it will be exactly what you need. For instance, I've had an old Edison light bulb and six oddly shaped pill boxes lying around for at least five years and so far I haven't found any use for them. Still, I haven't given up hope and thrown them away, and probably won't for at least another five years.

As for what you should save, that's up to you. I can only say that I've found a few categories of things that come in handy more often than others. Small, round objects, such as rubber balls, marbles and nuts, are particularly useful. Small, relatively flat things, such as sunflower seeds, make nice feet for very small dolls.

Never throw away a pair of nylons or pantyhose just because they have a run or two. They make excellent stuffing and they can be used to wrap wire bodies (Ch. 3). So can almost any material that is knit or stretchy, including men's socks and tee shirts.

Most kinds of wire, too, are a must. The only requirement is that it can be bent fairly easily. Those flimsy clothes hangers you get back from the laundry or dry cleaners may be just what you need. Heavier wire can be useful for really heavy or large wire body dolls.

Anything that is especially small and even remotely ornamental is another category to look for. This would include things such as sequins, stickpins, colorful buttons, snaps, eyelets and the little sword-shaped picks they put in mixed drinks. Sequins, since they come in all shapes and colors, are especially useful for very small dolls. I've used them for realistic looking buttons, purse decorations, and sheriffs' badges, just to mention a few.

Nonornamental items are useful, too, as long as they're small. The buckle from an old wristwatch strap, for instance, makes a good belt buckle; a couple of snaps from an old garter belt make passable straps for a pair of miniature bib overalls.

Finally, though it might seem a bit like cheating at first, there is nothing really wrong with cannibalizing bits and pieces from other dolls or doll houses. I don't do it often, but I find that I'm not above making occasional use of a miniature drinking glass, a tiny pair of shoes or even a wig. My conscience usually doesn't bother me more than a few seconds and in the end I usually decide my use was more imaginative than the original use anyway!

Chapter 2

*Basic Stitching
and
Working
with
Patterns*

If you have done any sewing at all, you can probably skip most of this chapter. It covers the basics, including the sort of thing that would inspire your average seamstress to say, "But *everyone* knows *that!*"

But not everyone does, as I have found out from the blank stares I've gotten occasionally from friends when I've shown them some of my dolls and made casual remarks about backstitches and overcasts.

So, if you have never done anything more complicated with a needle and thread than stitch a lumpy-edged patch on a pair of jeans, this chapter is for you. For the rest of you, who know how seams work and what backstitches and reduced patterns are, just flip through the pages and see if there's anything of interest to you. If there isn't, I'll see you again in Chapter 3, where we'll take up body building.

Sewing

NEEDLE AND THREAD

As I said, we'll start with the basics and nothing can be much more basic than threading a needle. Even someone who's never had a needle in his hand before will know enough to stick the thread through the eye. What happens after that, however, depends on whether you want to sew with a single or a double thread.

For a single thread, all you do is tie a knot in the "trailing end" of the thread to keep it from pulling through your fabric. The only problem with a single thread is that if you aren't careful, the thread could slip out of the needle.

For a double thread, tie the two ends of the thread together. A double thread gives you a stronger seam, and there's never any danger that the thread will slip out of the needle. There is, however, a definite danger that the thread will get twisted and tangled, in which case, unless you're terribly patient, you may have to cut the tangles open and start over. Tangles are much more likely with double thread than with single.

In most cases, you will probably want to use single thread. Most of the things you will be sewing are small, and you will have to keep the stitches pretty small, too. The only exception I can think of offhand are bodies that will have to be stuffed very tightly. For these, the stronger seams you get with double thread might help. On the other hand, a heavier, single thread would probably do just as well or better.

BASIC SEAMS

To make a basic seam, you simply place the two pieces of cloth with the *right sides of the fabric together*, facing in, and sew about a quarter of an inch in from the edges. A quarter-inch seam allowance is not standard, but is right for most doll garments. The line of stitching follows the outside edges of the fabric, whether straight or curved. Then, when you have finished the sewing, you turn the item inside out. This puts the right (print) side out, with the wrong (dull) side and all the ragged edges and stitches on the inside where they can't be seen. Thus, it is referred to throughout this book as "a standard *inside-out seam.*"

If you have any corners in the item you're sewing, you will have to cut off excess material before turning it right side out. Do this by cutting diagonally across the corners as shown in Figure 2–1. This will give you neat, square corners, as opposed to the lumpy ones you would get if you left the extra material in when you turned the item right side out.

The opposite problem is illustrated in Figure 2–2. If you turn a curved seam right side out without doing anything first, the material will not stretch

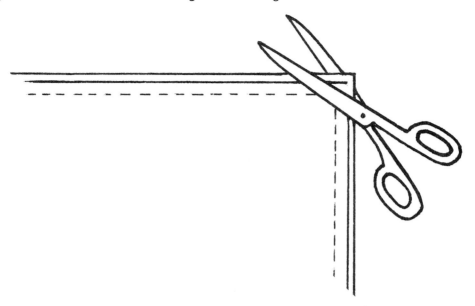

Fig. 2-1 Cutting excess material off corner seams for a neater finish.

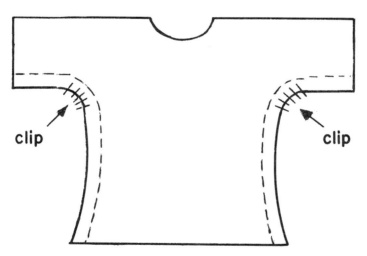

Fig. 2-2 Clipping curved seams from the wrong side of the fabric.

adequately; as a result, the fabric will pucker and pull. To avoid this, simply cut slits at several points in the curves, *up to*—but not through—your line of stitches. It helps substantially if you run a second row of stitches right on top of the first before you clip any points of stress.

Press all seams open on the wrong side after stitching. This sounds like an extra chore, but if everything lies completely flat you will find it much easier to join the pieces of a garment together. If also makes an amazing difference in the appearance of the finished garments—they're far more professional looking.

STITCHES

All the stitches you will need for anything in this book are shown in Figure 2–3.

RUNNING STITCH

If there is such a thing as a basic stitch, this is it. You simply run the needle back and forth through the fabric (Fig. 2–3A). To make the running stitch a bit neater and sturdier, go back over the row of stitches in the opposite direction, reversing the ins and outs, so that the line of stitching is completely covered with thread on both sides. Keeping the space between the stitches as equal as possible also contributes to the neatness. This is the basic stitch for which a sewing machine is most helpful.

When running stitches are made extremely large, it is called basting. Basting is usually the next step after pinning and it holds the pieces of fabric together while you do the real sewing with smaller stitches. The basting is pulled out when the seam is completed, so it's a good idea to baste with a contrasting color of thread so that it's easier to find and there's no danger of your pulling out the wrong thread. Basting stitches can be up to an inch long.

A long running stitch is also used to gather up fabric for ruffles or gathered skirts. Be sure to use strong thread for gathering, because if the thread breaks, you will have to start over from the beginning. You can't just pick up where you left off the way you can when the thread breaks in normal stitches.

BACKSTITCH

The backstitch is pretty much like the running stitch, except that each stitch overlaps the previous stitch (Fig. 2–3B). That is, each new stitch starts in back of where it would if you were using a running stitch. There are a variety of backstitches, but they are all basically the same stitch: the difference is simply in how much each stitch overlaps the last.

A backstitch done with heavy thread, such as embroidery floss, the color of which contrasts with the material being sewn, is called an outline stitch. It makes a nice, heavy line and is used mostly for decoration.

OVERCAST STITCH

This one, I suppose, is called "overcast" because the thread is literally cast over the edges of the fabric being sewn. As you can see in Figure 2–3C, it's somewhat like the binding in a spiral notepad. Though the overcast stitch makes a nicely finished edge on any fabric, it works especially well on heavy materials such as felt and leather. When you use this stitch, you do *not* have

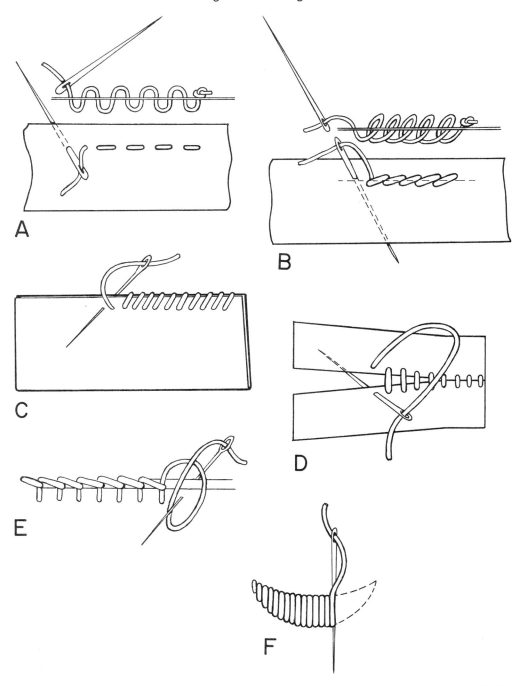

Fig. 2–3 Basic stitches. A: Running stitch. B: Backstitch. C: Overcast. D: Ladder stitch. E: Buttonhole. F: Satin stitch.

to turn the result inside out. That is, you start with the two wrong sides of the material facing each other, right sides of the fabric out, when you use this stitch. The overcast stitch is also good for trimming the edges of single thicknesses of material for hats, collars and cuffs.

LADDER STITCH

The ladder stitch is the same as the overcast, except that the two pieces of material are laid flat and butted up against each other, edge to edge. As you can see in Figure 2–3D, the stitch looks vaguely like a ladder.

The ladder stitch is used for fur, felt, leather or any fabric that needs to have the edges butted against each other rather than have a double thickness seam. The material, of course, has to be a type that doesn't ravel. The ladder stitch is useful if you need to have a completely flat surface where the two pieces of fabric are joined. On fur, especially, a standard "inside out" seam would be much too bulky.

BUTTONHOLE STITCH

The buttonhole is a sort of overlapping overcast. That is, it is the same as the overcast except that the thread is looped over the needle each time a stitch is taken (Figure 2–3E). The buttonhole stitch prevents ravelling and makes a fine, finished edge, better even than the overcast. Its primary use in normal sewing is, of course, in buttonholes, but we don't make very many buttonholes for dolls. Instead, we'll use it mostly for edging.

SATIN STITCH

The satin stitch is purely for decoration. It is an embroidery stitch used to fill in areas with solid color, such as eyes or mouths (Fig. 2–3F). In the satin stitch, unlike the other stitches, the thread must not be pulled tightly, because that destroys the shape of the area you are trying to fill and gives you nothing but a lump of puckered material. Try to pull the thread, floss or yarn just taut enough so that the material doesn't bend, yet each strand lies smoothly against the next.

CUTTING FABRIC

Cutting material is another of those basics that, although simple, has a few pitfalls. Most of them you would discover for yourself in short order, but perhaps a few words now can save you a few minutes or hours of wasted time later.

First, before you even do any cutting, make sure the material lies smoothly. If there are any wrinkles, take the time to press the material before you do anything else. If you're cutting material to a pattern, every little wrinkle will add a bit of width or length that you don't want and this is even more important in making doll clothes than it is in making clothing for yourself. It takes only a small deviation to alter the shape of a doll pattern: the half inch that a wrinkle or two might add to a standard pattern might not be noticed, but that same extra half inch in a doll pattern, which could be only a couple of inches wide to start with, would be most noticeable.

To cut to a pattern, simply lay the material out on a flat surface, pin the pattern to the fabric in several places and cut around the pattern. On everyday fabrics, such as cotton, use long, full strokes of the scissors. Besides being faster, this helps to avoid jagged edges.

On fur fabrics and felt, use short snips. (You probably wouldn't have the strength to cut that kind of fabric with long strokes, anyway.) On fur or fake fur, be careful not to cut through the hair itself, only the backing or hide. The best way to do this is to part the fur first, like you part the hair on your head, then cut right along the part. If the hair on the fur is too short to part, use a small embroidery scissors and slip the point of the scissors through the fur, close to the backing. In that way, you sort of part the fur as you cut. Leaving the hair intact allows it to fall over the seams, making them practically invisible.

Your scissors, of course, should be fairly sharp. If they're not sharp enough, the edges of the cloth come out ragged and full of ravels. When this happens, there's not much point in trying to get the scissors sharpened unless you have someone around the house who is handy at that sort of thing. The cost and trouble you'd have finding someone to do it right probably isn't worth it, especially since the scissors used for doll-size cutting needn't be all that expensive. The best thing to do is just buy another pair. In an emergency, you could sharpen scissors a little yourself by cutting sandpaper with them.

Be sure to keep old scissors; they are still perfectly good for cutting paper, which is something you should *never* do with new, sharp scissors. Cutting paper turns sharp, new scissors into dull, old scissors very rapidly.

Patterns

PLACEMENT AND CUTTING

As I mentioned briefly before, in order to cut fabric to a pattern you simply pin the pattern to the fabric and start cutting. The primary thing to be careful of is adequate *seam allowance* (see Basic Seams, earlier in this chapter). All the patterns in this book include seam allowances, but when you're using other patterns, always make sure before you start cutting. If it isn't included, provide for your own seam allowance by cutting about a quarter of an inch out from the pattern edges as shown in Figure 2–4; thus, your *cutting line* is always a quarter of an inch beyond your *stitching line*.

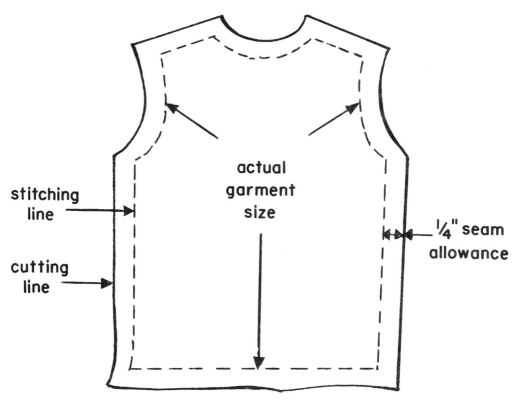

stitching
line

cutting
line

actual
garment
size

¼" seam
allowance

Fig. 2–4 Gauging the correct seam allowance by
checking cutting line and stitching line.

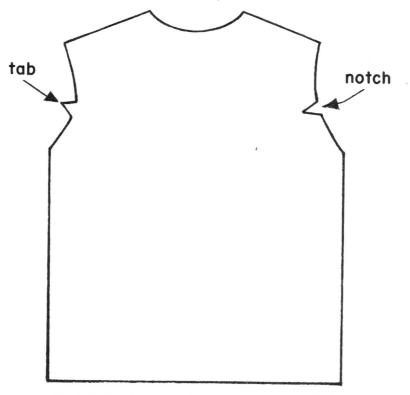

tab

notch

Fig. 2–5 Notches and tabs on pattern pieces help in
matching fabric parts of a garment.

Most patterns include *notches:* markers to show you just how to match up the different pieces to be sewn together (Fig. 2–5). It's sort of like putting pencil marks on a couple of boards to show where they're to be nailed together. They are called notches, I suppose, because that's what they look like in most patterns. It's more practical, however, to make tabs, or inside-out-notches, as shown in Figure 2–5. Tabs are easier to find and line up with each other, for one thing. For another, it eliminates the danger of getting them too big and cutting so far into the material that you cut through the seam line.

You will find that many of the pattern pieces in this book carry the notation *"fold"* along one or more edges: this simply means to place the pattern piece on a double thickness of material, positioning that specific edge where the fabric is folded. In this manner, you cut two garment pieces simultaneously; for example, the front and back of a shirt that does not have to be seamed across the shoulders, thus eliminating extra sewing.

Also, pay special attention as you work to instructions on the patterns, transferring such directions as *gather* or *fold line* and markings for pleats and darts to the fabric (very lightly on the wrong side of the material, with soft pencil or chalk).

ENLARGING AND REDUCING PATTERNS

Because of space limitations, most of the patterns in this book are reduced. All such patterns are pictured on a grid. The size of the grid squares may appear to vary from pattern to pattern, depending on the amount of reduction, but all were drawn on a 1-inch grid. To enlarge any one of these patterns to full size, all you have to do is copy them square by square onto graph paper with 1-inch squares. The grid squares simply serve as an easy reference and make it quite simple to enlarge the pattern.

If you make any original patterns of your own and plan to ever enlarge or reduce them, you can make it as easy as possible for yourself by drawing them on graph paper and lining up the straight edges of the patterns with the lines on the graph. An example of an enlarged and reduced pattern is shown in Figure 2–6.

One problem you may have with a few of the patterns in this book is that, because of the nature of the dolls, "full size" may not always be truly full size. For example, the precise size of the clothes for the wishbone doll (Ch. 8) will depend on the exact size of the wishbone you use. Thus, you will probably have to do a little further enlarging or reducing once you get your "full size" pattern drawn. Also, you may want to vary the size of the doll yourself. That is, the size of most of the dolls in this book is determined by the size of the head. A particularly large gourd (Ch. 9), for instance, would require a larger body than the one I used.

There are a couple of methods suitable for enlarging or reducing a pattern

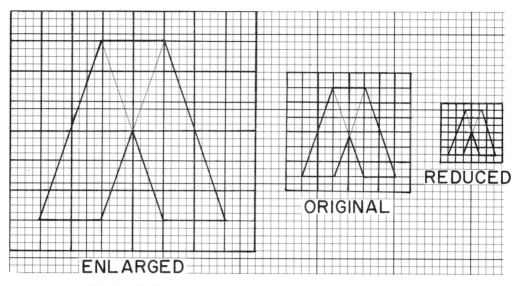

Fig. 2–6 Enlarging or reducing patterns by using graph paper.

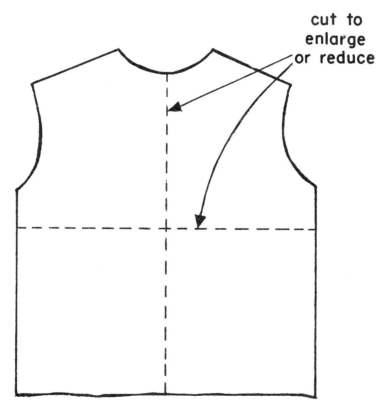

Fig. 2–7 Altering garment size by cutting a pattern piece
into sections.

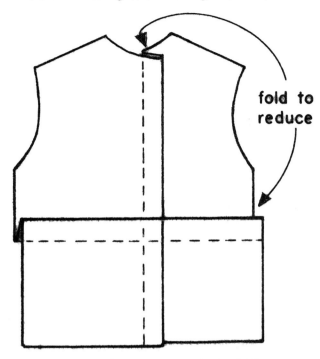

fold to reduce

Fig. 2-8   Reducing garment size by folding a
pattern piece.

if the change is relatively slight. One is illustrated in Figure 2-7. In this
method, you simply cut the pattern down the middle in both directions and
then move the four quarters of the pattern either together (to reduce) or apart
(to enlarge). Once you have them positioned the way you want, fasten them to
another piece of paper, cut around them, and you have your altered pattern.
For reduction, you needn't cut the pattern at all if you don't want to. Instead,
you can fold it along the two center lines as shown in Figure 2-8. This makes
the pattern easier to restore to its original size.

The main problem with either method is that the pattern will become
distorted if the change is very great. For instance, in the shirt pattern shown in
Figures 2-7 and 2-8, the cut for the neck changes size but the cuts for the
sleeve holes do not. If you shrank it too much, the neck cut would disappear
altogether.

For very slight changes in size, it may not be necessary to make a different
size pattern at all. Just use your original pattern and make the seam allowances
a little larger or a little smaller. A pattern for a 10-inch doll, for instance, could
be used for a 9- or 11-inch doll this way. But don't try it for changes much
greater than that. Things will get distorted even more quickly this way than in
the cutting and folding method.

MAKING ORIGINAL PATTERNS

Dolls are relatively easy to make patterns for. For one thing, they're small. For another, they don't squirm and giggle while you're pinning things on them. They just lie there, inert and cooperative.

First, lay the finished doll on a piece of paper and draw an outline around it. Don't trace closely around the edges, but make your lines at least a half inch out from the body at all points. Or, if you want to be more precise, pull the paper up on each side of the doll and make your marks where the side seams in the clothes will be.

This outline gives you a starting point for the pattern. It will serve primarily as a size guide. As for the patterns for the individual pieces (shirt front, shirt sleeve, etc.), these are basic and can be picked up from any standard pattern. That is, you can use the outline you have just drawn, together with the basic shapes from any standard pattern, to make a "trial pattern" for your specific doll. Cut your trial pattern out of paper towelling, the sturdier the better. You will be doing a lot of pinning and pulling before you've gotten the trial pattern into final shape; you don't want it to fall apart before you're done.

Next, take the pieces of paper towel trial pattern and fit them onto the doll as best you can. You can either hold the pieces on the doll with your fingers (if you're very dextrous) or pin them on. Whatever you do, *don't use tape!* Tape will only tear the toweling when you try to take it off.

Once you have the pieces on the doll, start experimenting. Make folds and darts here and there, cut off excess towelling, replace too-small pieces with larger ones, etc. Then, when the trial pattern fits fairly well, take the pieces off the doll, flatten them out, and trace around them onto a piece of paper. For seam allowance, draw another line about $\frac{1}{4}$-inch out from the one you have just drawn. The outside line is the shape of your final pattern for cutting.

To put notches or tabs on your pattern, put the cut-out paper parts together and draw notches on the parts that come together. If your patterns are fairly simple or if you have an excellent memory, the notches may not be necessary. It's usually a good idea to include them, though, just to avoid confusion later.

It is easiest if you make a complete pattern for a doll before you start working on the fabric itself. Just be sure to label all the pieces of the pattern as soon as you're done. Write on each piece what part it is (shirt front, sleeve, etc.) and what doll it is for. Then put each completed pattern into a separate envelope. If you make very many patterns—like more than one or two—you will be surprised, not to mention annoyed, at how murky your memory becomes when you start looking for a specific pattern next year or next month or even, if you're like me, the day after tomorrow.

Making your own patterns takes a little practice and patience, like everything else, but it doesn't require a lot of skill. And don't worry if the patterns or the fabric don't end up looking all smooth and professional. You can always sew a few tucks in the finished garments to make them fit better. Besides, homemade dolls aren't supposed to look all that slick. If you don't have a few rough edges and afterthoughts here and there, no one will believe that you made them all by yourself.

Chapter 3

All-Purpose Wire Bodies

Although we will use a number of different kinds of bodies, there is one kind which is used so often and can be used for so many different dolls, that it deserves a chapter of its own. This is the wire armature body or, more simply, "wire body."

The wire body is certainly the most versatile, as well as one of the most durable and easiest to use. For one thing, it can be used with almost any kind of head. For another, it is one of the easiest to make. My own chief reason for liking it is the fact that it is flexible enough to bend, yet stiff enough to hold any shape I give it. This allows me to position the completed doll any way I want—standing up, sitting down, crawling, anything—and I can change it as often as I want. In fact, finding things for the dolls to do, places to put them and ways to arrange groups of them could become another hobby all by itself.

Pipe Cleaner Body

The simplest type of wire body is made from a couple of pipe cleaners. Although these can be used as frames for very small dolls, more often, they serve as the entire body. The figure on the right in Figure 3–1, for example, is little more than a naked pipe cleaner painted black, with an acorn for a head, a bit of felt for a bow tie and a pair of sunflower seeds for feet.

To make a pipe cleaner body such as either of the ones in Figure 3–1, you need two pipe cleaners. Start by folding one of the cleaners in half: this one will be the trunk and legs. The folded end will be stuck into whatever you use for a head.

The second cleaner, cut to a length about half or two thirds that of the first, can be used for arms. Simply twist it once around the neck portion of the body, leaving enough of the neck sticking through so that a head can be fastened onto it. If you can't twist the arms tightly enough to hold them steady, add a drop of glue.

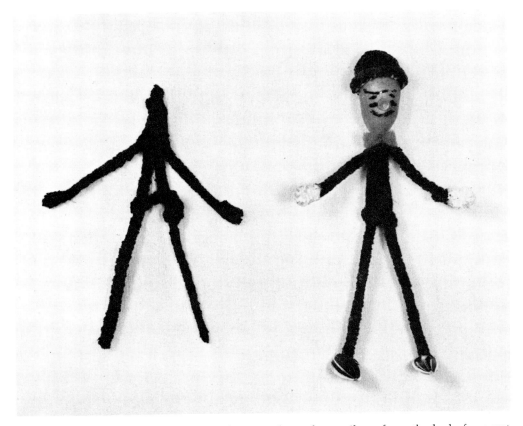

Fig. 3–1 A couple of pipe cleaners can be twisted together easily to form the body for a nut head character.

Finally, cut approximately one inch from the leftover part of the second cleaner. Determine where on the first cleaner you want the hips to be, then space the legs so they are a quarter to a half inch apart at the hips. The inch-long section is used to form the hips and to keep the legs the proper distance apart: keep the center section of the inch-long piece straight and twist each end around one of the legs at hip level (Fig. 3–1). Squeeze the loops down as tightly as you can with pliers. As with the arms, a bit of glue can be added if necessary. If you wish, the ends of the arms can be looped to form hands and the ends of the legs bent at right angles to form feet.

Wrapped Wire Body

For larger, more elaborate dolls, the wrapped wire body is often used. A body of this type, before and after the wrapping, is shown in Figure 3–2; a partially wrapped wire doll is shown in Figure 11–1. It is more time consuming to make than the pipe cleaner body, but the basic principle is the same; because of the larger size, it can actually be easier to make.

Fig. 3–2   The twisted wire structure (left) is wrapped with strips of nylon stocking to pad out the body.

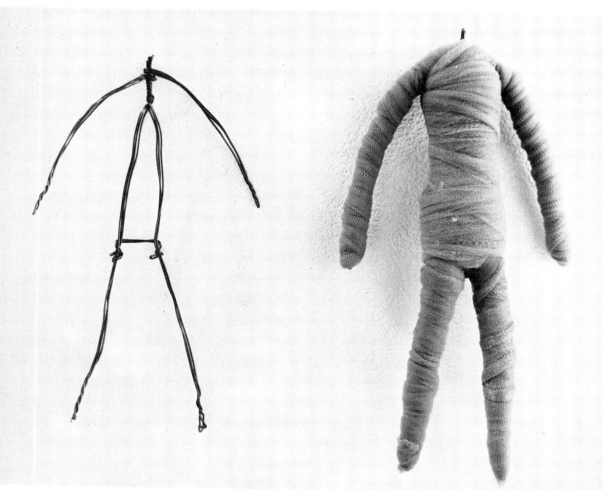

The biggest problem may be to find wire of the right thickness, and this you will have to do by trial and error. What the right thickness is depends on the kind of pliers you have to bend it with, how strong you are and how much practice you've had. A starting point might be the flimsiest clothes hanger you have in the house. If that's too heavy, check the local hardware store; copper wire is more pliable, and a few cents' worth should be enough for several bodies. On the other hand, if the only wire you have on hand is too thin—jewelry wire, for instance—you can twist a number of separate strands together and use that. The bare one in Figure 3–2 was made this way.

Once you have the wire, decide how long the body should be. For adult dolls, the bodies are normally six or seven times the height of the head. For small children, the bodies will be only about four times the height of the head. Most of the types of doll heads discussed throughout this book are suitable for wrapped wire bodies.

The trunk and leg section is made the same way the pipe cleaner body was made. Cut a length of wire roughly twice the length you want the body to be, then fold it in half. To make a neck, twist the folded end two or three times. This twist is a good test to see if you have the right thickness of wire. If you can twist it by hand, it's probably too light. If you can't twist it even with your pliers, you either need thinner wire or help from a friend with stronger fingers.

Next, cut a piece of wire for the arms, roughly equal in length to the length of the body, i.e., half the length of the first wire. Wrap this once or twice around the bottom of the neck twist: pinch it down as tightly as you can, but don't worry if it's a little loose. The wrapping you will be putting on will hold it in place.

The final piece of wire for forming the hips should be about half as long as one of the arms. Locate the point at which you want the legs to start, and space them as far apart as you want them to be. Now use the short piece of wire to fix them in place. Keeping the center section of the short piece straight, twist the ends around each of the legs at the hips. Squeeze the twists down tightly so that the hip wire won't slide down the legs before you get the frame wrapped. It should now look somewhat like the form on the left in Figure 3–2.

Next is the wrapping: I normally use old nylon stockings or pantyhose, although any knitted, stretchy material will work. Old tee shirts or men's socks work just as well and give you more color selection. Whatever you are using, cut it into long strips about 1½ inches wide. If you're using nylons, cut off the tops (the more opaque portions) but don't throw them away. Then, starting at the top of the nylon, cut *diagonally* down and around, so that you end up with a single, continuous strip. Just keep cutting until you have used up the whole thing, heel, toe and all. Whatever you use, try to cut it in a similar way, ending up with the longest possible single strip.

For the actual wrapping, there are a number of things that should be pointed out. Leave the neck twist bare, so it can be poked into and glued to the head. Do the whole body at once, not a part at a time. That is, if you start winding the first strip around one of the arms, go across to the other arm, back to the body, down the body, down one leg, etc. Keep going this way, back and forth across all parts of the body except the neck twist, until you have it the way you want it.

Make the wrappings fairly tight. To do this, of course, you will have to stretch the strips as you wind them, and they will tend to get narrower and curl in at the edges. This is perfectly all right; there's no reason to keep them flat as you wind them. In fact, it won't do any noticeable damage if you accidentally make a twist or two in the strips.

To make the first strip easier to start, anchor it by poking a hole near the end of the strip and sticking the neck twist or an arm or leg through the hole. Then, as you near the end of each strip, fasten the beginning of the next strip to the end of the previous one with a couple of stitches.

To pad out the places that need to be fatter, you can either keep on adding more strips in those places or you can pad them out with cotton or rag stuffing.

When the body is the size and shape you want, take a stitch or two into the end of the last strip to keep the whole thing from unravelling. As you can see in Figure 3–2, the completed body looks vaguely like an Egyptian mummy. If you wish, you can add some "skin" by cutting pieces from the leftover translucent stocking tops and sewing them in place over the arms and legs.

Chapter 4

Distinctive Wigs and Fabulous Faces

In this chapter, I'll discuss the options you have for those all-important touches that make your doll an original. Making a wig or applying facial features can be done easily and quickly, or you can make a real project out of it—it all depends on two things: what's right for the individual doll and your own creative inclinations. Later in this chapter, you'll find a section on accessories: how to make purses, pompoms and a myriad of beribboned accents. This is only the beginning, however; when you start to put the finishing touches to your own dolls, you will probably think of any number of variations you want to try.

Wigs and Other Hairy Subjects

As with people, the type of hair you want depends on the type of head you have. Some dolls, like some men, look better without any hair at all, while others will look best with a real crowning glory.

On nuts and other solid heads, for instance, paint will do quite well. Rag and soft dolls, on the other hand, usually look better with yarn or thread wigs. I'll explain how to make several types of wigs and a variety of hairstyles, none really too difficult. In the chapters on individual types of dolls, I'll make some recommendations as to what type of hair to use, but remember that they're only recommendations, not orders. If you have other ideas—and I hope you will—let them loose and see what happens.

PAINTED HAIR

Painted hair is the easiest kind to make: on many of the nut and carved head dolls, it is also the most effective. "Real" hair, in fact, could just get in the way in the case of many of the nuts. Hickory nuts, for example, have a shape that looks quite hairy when enhanced by paint. And acorns, of course, have their own built-in caps, so for them you don't even need the paint.

I usually start by making a pencil sketch on the doll's head, showing roughly what the hair will look like. This serves a double purpose. First, it is a pattern for the painting itself. Second, if you decide you don't like the style, the pencil marks are easier to wipe off than paint. When you have the pattern and style you want, just go ahead and paint.

For dolls that children will play with, I always use acrylic paint just to be on the safe side. For other dolls I prefer oil paints, which have a number of advantages. For one thing, they are quite thick and won't run of their own accord. Thus you can do quite a few things with them that you couldn't do with thinner, runnier paints. For instance, if you put the paint on fairly thickly, you can make brushstroke lines through it to give it a realistic, hairy texture. After the first coat has dried, you can put in highlights and shadows by adding streaks of lighter or darker paint.

Oil paints take quite a long time to dry completely, from a day up to a whole week, depending on the humidity and the thickness of the paint. You might think that this slow drying is a disadvantage, but it is often just the opposite. For one thing, you can blend oil paints very easily while they are still somewhat wet and this quality comes in handy fairly often, particularly if you're indecisive. Say, for example, you've painted white hair on a granny-type nut and now, after looking at it, you decide the white is too stark or severe. You can change the color to gray by adding a smidgin of black paint. Just put the black on right over the white, then brush back and forth. Pretty soon the two colors will blend and you will have your gray color in a matter of minutes.

The thickness of the oil paints also comes in handy if you want to give a doll a fashionably frosted look. After the initial color has dried, put a small blob of another color paint where you want the streaks to begin. Then stick the brush into the blob and drag the bristles wherever you want the streaks to go. Again because of the slow drying, if you don't like your first streaks, you can wipe them off with a tissue and start over.

FUR WIGS

Another simple way to make hair is to use a scrap of fur. Three such scraps are shown in Figure 4–1: the end ones are rabbit; the one in the middle is Persian lamb (also known as Caracul) and it makes an excellent wig if you trim it neatly and fasten it down properly. You wouldn't want to run out and buy a piece of this fur from a furrier, though; it would cost half a fortune. What you do is check the Goodwill-type stores, where I've occasionally found a Persian lamb collar for less than a dollar. Or you might even be lucky enough to find one lying around in your attic on Grandma's old coat.

The only problem with fur wigs is that they won't stand much washing. I remember having a doll with a fur wig once, back when I was a little girl a century or so ago. It was a fabulous rubber baby doll with a lamb's wool wig when I got it. Unfortunately, I must have been an exceptionally clean child, because I gave the doll a bath at every opportunity. It only took a few months of that kind of treatment before the skin on the wig became hard and started coming loose. It wasn't long before I was left with a bald doll! I've seen similar dolls since then, just as old but in excellent condition. They probably just didn't belong to cleaning freaks like me.

To make a fur wig, it's helpful to make a pattern first. Start by cutting a circle of paper big enough to cover the part of the doll's head that you want the hair to cover. Next, place the paper circle on the doll's head and press down until you have made a sort of cap. You now have a circle of paper full of

Fig. 4–1 Small scraps of fur can be used to make doll wigs. The one in the center is Persian lamb, with two rabbit coiffures shown.

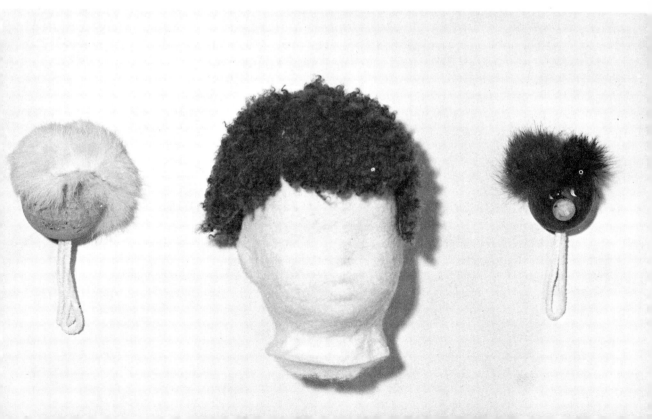

creases and folds. Take the circle, flatten it out and mark where all the creases and folds were. Next, lay the flattened circle on a piece of fur and cut around it.

Finally, make little folds in the fur circle to match the folds in the paper pattern. Sew the folds in place and you have the beginnings of your fur wig. Before you cut off any excess material from the folds, however, try the wig on the doll. If you cut the material off first and then find the wig doesn't quite fit, there's not much you can do about it.

When the shaped fur fits satisfactorily, cut the excess from under the folds and glue the wig on the head with white glue. Let the glue set fairly well, then trim around the edges of the wig to get the precise shape you want. Be sure that the glue is *almost* dry before you start trimming. If you start too soon, the wig will slide around and be very difficult to trim. With the glue properly set, you can still lift up the edges enough to trim where you wish, while the rest of the wig stays put. Once you have the wig in the desired shape, poke a little more glue under the lifted edges with a cotton swab and press the wig back down. Any stray hair can be trimmed off later.

If you're lucky enough to find some long-haired fur, such as racoon or bear, you could part it and style the wig almost like human hair. Very long-haired fake fur might work, too.

BASIC YARN SKEIN WIGS

There are many ways to make wigs from yarn and thread. The simplest makes use of a skein of yarn. For extremely large dolls, say 20 inches tall or taller, you can use a complete 4-ounce skein of yarn, the kind you can buy at almost any department, variety or fabric store. For smaller dolls, you will have to wind your own skeins, the length of the loops depending on how large the doll is and how long you want the hair to be. For very small dolls, one or two dozen loops of heavy thread only a few inches long will be enough. The clothespin doll in Chapter 5, for instance, uses one about that size.

The basic method of making a skein wig is shown in Figure 4–2. You simply lay the skein out flat, trying to keep the loops fairly evenly distributed and then sew directly across the center of the skein as shown. To make a wig a little sturdier or to make it so it can be glued to a solid head as well as stitched to a stuffed head, use a strip of cloth or bias tape under the stitching line for reinforcement. This is shown by the dashed line in Figure 4–2A; it can be included before the first stitching across the yarn is done or it can be added later.

It's best to use a machine for this stitching, though it would be possible to do it by hand if you have a lot of patience. If you have trouble keeping the yarn evenly distributed as you feed it through the machine, you could try putting a length of tape on each side of the line along which you are going to

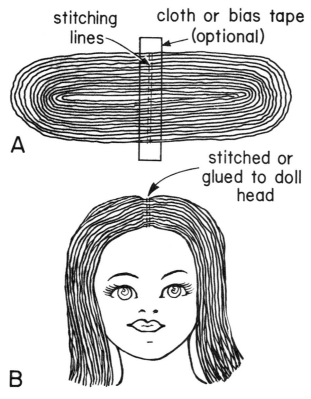

stitching lines cloth or bias tape (optional)

A

stitched or glued to doll head

B

Fig. 4–2 Basic yarn skein wig. A: The stitching line is reinforced with bias tape. B: Stitching or gluing the wig to the head.

stitch. Keep the tape an inch or so away from the actual line of stitching, though, and make sure the tape you use won't leave half its stickiness behind on the yarn when you pull it off after sewing. Regular cellophane tape, for instance, doesn't work very well, but masking tape or the newer "magic" tapes are fine.

Once you have stitched across the skein as shown, simply sew the wig to the head along the same stitching line (Fig. 4–2B). A backstitch works best for fastening the wig to the head. Figure 4–3 shows four of the hairstyles that can be made using the yarn skein wig.

BUN

The bun (Fig. 4–3A) is the simplest and easiest to make: pull the ends of the loops together at the back of the head, then gently twist the yarn and wrap the loops in a circle. Don't cut any of the loops. A few stitches here and there with matching yarn will hold the bun in place once it's arranged the way you want.

Fig. 4–3 Yarn hairstyles. A: Bun. B: Braids. C: Curls. D: Bob.

BRAIDS

To make braids (Fig. 4–3B), start by pulling the yarn ends out from the head until they lie straight, then cut through the loops so that you are left with individual strands, all the same length, Next, to keep the doll from looking bald in back, arrange the yarn so that it covers the whole head, then use matching yarn to take a few stitches all around the edge where the hairline would be. Again, a backstitch works best for this. Also, unless you want a very severe looking hairstyle, be careful not to pull the yarn too tight before stitching: leave the strands fairly loose and fluffy. After stitching around the hairline, simply divide the loose strands below the hairline and make braids.

CURLS

To make the glorious curls shown in Figure 4–3C, begin by clipping the yarn loops the same as you do for the braids. Next, determine where you want the curls to start, i.e., at the hairline, halfway up toward the top of the head or wherever. Then stitch the yarn to the head at that point, just as you did for the braids; arrange the yarn to cover the back of the head before you stitch it.

To form each set of curls, wrap a dozen or so strands of yarn around a pencil. Start wrapping at the head end and wrap out along the pencil. (Wrapping in the other direction by rolling the yarn up on the pencil would probably end up in a tangle.) When you have the curl formed, put a couple of bobby pins in it to hold the shape and then remove the pencil.

How to set the curl depends on the kind of yarn you have. If you're using plain wool or an acrylic yarn, simply dampen the curls a little with your wet fingertips. For mohair or angora yarns, which are somewhat more delicate and prettier than wool, give the curls a short shot of steam from a spray steam iron. Be sure that you don't actually iron the curls flat; just spray the steam on the curls as they hang in the air.

After drying a few hours, the curls will be set and you can remove the bobby pins (be careful not to pull any strands of yarn out of the curl). If you wish, you can use matching yarn to stitch a part of each curl to the head to hold it in place.

For a curl that is very permanent but rather harsh to the touch, you can mix a little white glue in the water you use to set the curls. You can't, of course, use this with the mohair or angora yarn. For one thing, the glue wouldn't do the steam iron any good; for another, the glue would make the yarn look stringy and you would lose all the natural hair effect.

For less neat looking curls, you can simply use old yarn—some that you've unravelled from a knitted sweater, for example. Such used yarn will be all kinky and will make great, if disorganized, curls. Just wind the yarn loosely into a skein the same way you would with new yarn, then stitch and fasten to the head the same way you did for the basic yarn skein wig. Be careful not to wind the skein so tightly that you pull out the kinks.

BOB

There are a couple of ways to make a bob hairstyle. The simplest way is to arrange the yarn of the skein wig so that it evenly covers not only the back and sides of the head, but the front as well. Stitch it into place at the hairline and then simply cut the yarn straight around the head, as if you were giving someone an old fashioned bowl haircut.

Making a bob exactly like the illustration (Fig. 4–3D), isn't really that much more complicated. In this one, the bangs are made separately and are fastened to the head before the skein wig is attached. In that way, the stitching which attaches the bangs to the head is covered by the rest of the wig.

To make the bangs, lay out a few dozen strands of yarn or thread, all slightly longer than you want the bangs to be. Then stitch across the yarn near one end, as shown in Figure 4–4A; you can use some bias tape for reinforcement if you wish. Next, stitch the bangs to the head as indicated, being careful to place the bangs so that the stitches and bias tape will be hidden by the rest of the wig when it is added (Fig. 4–4B).

Another way to make a bob without making separate bangs is shown in Figure 4–5. It is just a slight variation on the basic yarn skein wig. Instead of sewing down the middle of the skein, sew across it fairly near one end, the shorter end being your allowance for the bangs (Fig. 4–5A). Then fasten it to the head with the stitching line running sideways (Fig. 4–5B). Cut the loops on the forehead and you have the bangs. With this type of wig, though, you aren't limited to a bob hairstyle. You could make a boy's traditional (i.e., relatively short) style out of it. To do that, arrange the yarn evenly over the head and use matching yarn to stitch it to the head about where the hairline would normally be. Then clip the yarn off just a little below that line. If you leave the bangs fairly long in front, you can brush the yarn to one side to make it look more natural.

SPIRAL YARN WIGS

The spiral yarn wig is a distant relative of the skein wigs and is used on soft or stuffed doll heads. It gives you an Orphan Annie style and you can make it as short or long as you want.

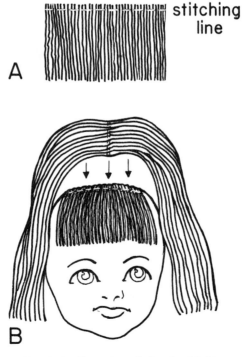

Fig. 4-4 Two-piece bob. A: Making separate bangs. B: Fitting the parts on the doll's head.

stitch

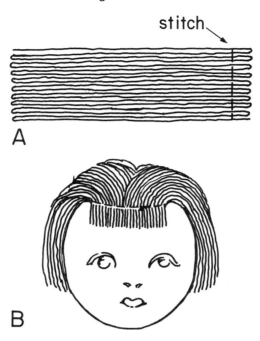

A

B

Fig. 4–5 One-piece bob. A: Stitching the
yarn. B: Fastening the wig to the doll's head.

To make a spiral wig, start with a strip of heavy paper, say about a yard
long and two inches wide. Two or three thicknesses of rolled newspaper is
about the right weight. As for length, I say a yard because it's an easy size to
handle and it will be long enough for any but the very largest dolls. The width
depends on how long or "deep" you want the hair to be. The 2-inch strip will
give you a hair depth of up to about ¾ inch.

Wind the yarn continuously around and around the strip of paper until
completely covered. As you wind, lay the strands of yarn next to one another
rather loosely. If some get overlapped, don't worry about it, but generally try to
keep the yarn in a single layer. A 1-yard strip will take about half of a 4-ounce
skein of yarn.

Once the winding is complete, sew right down the center of the strip,
preferably with a close machine stitch. The stitching not only fastens the yarn
loops together, but also perforates the paper, allowing you to remove the paper
without much trouble. If you want to reinforce the stitches after removing the
paper, sew the yarn to a length of bias tape or a cloth strip.

To sew the wig to the doll's head, place one end of the strip of yarn at
about the center of the area to be covered—approximately where a cowlick
would be. Wind the yarn strip around and around in a spiral, moving out from
the starting point as shown in Figure 4–6. The depth of the resulting hair is
determined by how wide the strip was and how close together you place the

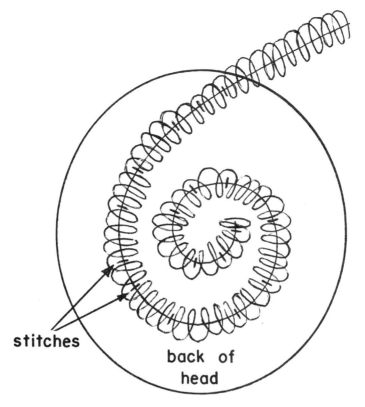

Fig. 4-6 Attaching the finished spiral yarn wig to
the head.

successive spirals. The more closely the spiral is spaced, the straighter the yarn
loops will stand up and the deeper the hair will be.

LOTSA-LOOPS YARN HAIRSTYLES

Lotsa-loop hair comes closer to being actual hair than most because each
strand is fastened directly to the head. It is also the most time consuming to
make, though it's not particularly difficult.

To make this type, all you have to do is sew, and sew, and sew—and sew
some more. Instead of using thread to fasten the yarn to the head, use a
darning needle and use the yarn itself as thread. Take a stitch with the yarn;
then, instead of pulling the stitch down flat onto the head, put your finger
under the yarn to form a loop. Go on to another stitch, another loop, another
stitch, etc., as indicated in Figure 4-7. Just keep repeating all over the head,
making the stitches close enough together to keep any of the bare head from
showing through.

This type of hair is the best to use for dolls that will be played with by
small children, who tend to stick anything and everything into their mouths.

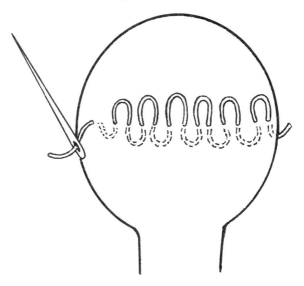

Fig. 4–7 The lotsa-loops yarn wig is made by
stitching the yarn directly onto a stuffed doll
head.

There is very little possibility of the yarn pulling loose and no strands are long enough for a child to choke on.

A similar method, illustrated in Figure 4–8, can be used to make curls. The advantage to this method is that you can make a half dozen or so curls for each stitch. Again, you use a darning needle with the yarn threaded through it. In this method, you take a stitch with the yarn, wrap the yarn loosely around a pencil several times and take a second stitch to anchor the other end of the curl to the head. Then, with both ends of the curl stitched down, run the needle back through the inside of the loops, next to the pencil, and take a final stitch back at the first end of the curl. (Without the yarn running back down the center of the curl this way, the curl would come unraveled the minute the pencil came out, leaving you with nothing but a very large loop of yarn.) Finally, remove the pencil and go on to your next curl.

Faces

PAINTED FEATURES

The faces on solid heads—like nuts and wood—are nearly always painted on and the shape and texture of the head often dictate what kind of face you want. Certain nuts, for instance, may remind you of particular types of people or even of specific individuals. A perfectly round ball might look like a baby or a fat man, for example.

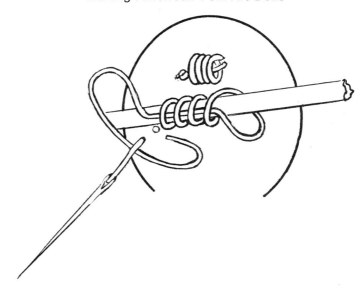

Fig. 4–8 Lotsa-loops curls are sewn directly onto the doll's head with yarn, using a pencil for wrapping.

As with painted hair, draw your faces on first with pencil so you can wipe off any mistakes easily. For babies' faces, cluster all features below the center of the object you're using for a head. For adults, place the nose at the center and leave the forehead of normal proportions. It is easier, of course, to make cartoon faces rather than to try to make realistic faces. Often a few suggestive lines are all you will need and sometimes you can take advantage of the natural shape of the object. This is particularly true of the nuts (see Ch. 7) and the gourds (see Ch. 9).

As for the type of paint to use, the same cautions apply here as for the hair. Model paint is very good, drying quickly to a high sheen, but acrylic is safer if the dolls are going to be used by small children.

EMBROIDERED FACES

Faces can either be painted or embroidered on fabric dolls. Usually it is easier to apply the features before stuffing, while the fabric is still flat. On knit or stretchy material, however, you had better wait until the doll is completed. The thread or paint will not stretch as much as the fabric and you could end up with a face that is either puckered or cracked. In most cases, I prefer embroidery to painting. For one thing, the thread won't hurt a child if she sticks it in her mouth and the embroidered face won't be hurt, either. Another advantage is that the thread colors are permanent and won't come off or bleed into the fabric around it.

When embroidering, I like to use three strands of the standard six-strand embroidery floss. The full six strands are a little too bulky, particularly for smaller dolls. To split the floss in two, just cut off whatever length you will need for sewing, separate the strands at one end, and simply take three strands in each hand and pull gently until the entire length is separated. To keep it from tangling, you might have to use something (like maybe your teeth) to hold the six-strand end steady. If you don't have any embroidery floss, three strands of regular sewing thread will work about as well.

Decorative Accents

SHOES

Shoes can be made of almost anything. For a pipe cleaner man, sunflower seeds, flat side down, make decorative and effective footwear. The natural stripes give them a sporty look, but they can be painted a solid color if you choose. On rag dolls, shoes can be sewn or painted right on the legs and if you want to make them look old fashioned, just paint or sew tiny buttons on the sides.

Separate shoes can be constructed of almost any material, but my own favorites are felt and leather. They don't fray and they don't need to be bound around the edges or lined. Any leather you use, of course, will have to be rather thin and supple, like deer hide or suede. I usually make my shoes from pieces of old gloves.

The basic parts for constructing a shoe are shown in Figure 4–9, along with a sketch of a finished shoe. The first step, regardless of the material you use, is to form the upper section of the shoe and stitch the two ends together, using a ladder stitch. If you use felt or some lighter material, you should then be able to sew the top of the shoe directly onto the sole. If you use leather, however, you may have to punch holes in the leather first; using a leather punch or anything else that has a sharp enough point, space holes evenly around the edge. Place the top section of the shoe onto the sole and mark through the holes onto the top of the sole using anything that will make a good indentation, such as the lead of a sharp pencil. Finally, punch the holes at the indicated spots around the edge of the sole and stitch the two parts together.

If you want to make the shoes a little sturdier, you could use the glove stitch when fastening the two parts together. The glove stitch is the same as the overcast stitch (see Ch. 2), except that you run the needle through each hole twice.

PURSES

Purses are probably the easiest of all accessories to make. You simply take two pieces of material—rectangles or circles or any shape you want—and sew them together. Then add a small strip of material for a strap and there you are.

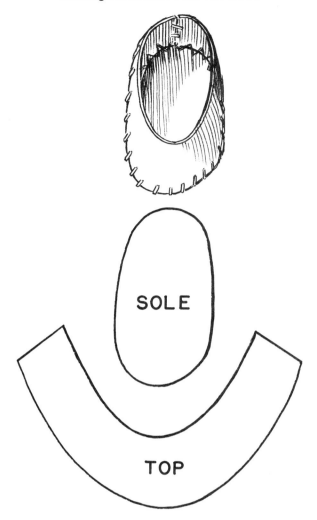

Fig. 4–9 Standard pattern for doll shoes can be
used with fabric or leather.

Or you can use a single circular piece of material to make a pouch style purse.
To do that, you simply hem the circle all around and then run a drawstring
inside the casing. Pull the string up tight to form the pouch, and the drawstring
becomes a strap as well.

   To make the purses distinctive and individual, all sorts of decorations,
such as beads, embroidery, rickrack, emblems, etc., can be added. A number of
typical purses are shown in Figure 4–10.

POMPOMS

   Pompoms are the fuzzy yarn balls that decorate many children's caps and
string ties. They are quite simple to make and you can use them not only for
decorations, but make entire dolls out of them! All you need to make the

Fig. 4–10 Ribbons, purses and corsages are some of the accessories you'll want to make for your dolls.

menagerie shown in the color section, Figures 6 and 15, are some different colored yarns, a bobby pin, a couple of metal or cardboard washers, and a little imagination.

The steps in making a pompom are outlined in Figure 4–11. Start with a pair of washers about an inch and a half in diameter. I use that dimension because anything much smaller would have too small a center hole to work well. The resulting pompom is also about an inch and a half in diameter and that is large enough for most decorations. You can always trim the pompoms to make them smaller.

Take a piece of yarn about two yards long and thread one end through a bobby pin, just as if it were a needle. Next, place the two washers together with the other end of the yarn anchored tightly between them. Using the bobby pin for a needle, wind the yarn tightly around the two washers as shown (Fig. 4–11A). Continue winding until the washers are completely covered. To make fuller pompoms, just go around the washers more than once, until the hole in the center is filled with yarn.

Carefully cut through all the strands of yarn around the outer edge, between the two washers, as shown (Fig. 4–11B). If the center holes are fairly full, the yarn will stay in place after cutting. When the cutting is complete, take a matching piece of yarn about eight inches long and slide it down between the washers (Fig. 4–11C). Wrap it tightly around the yarn between the

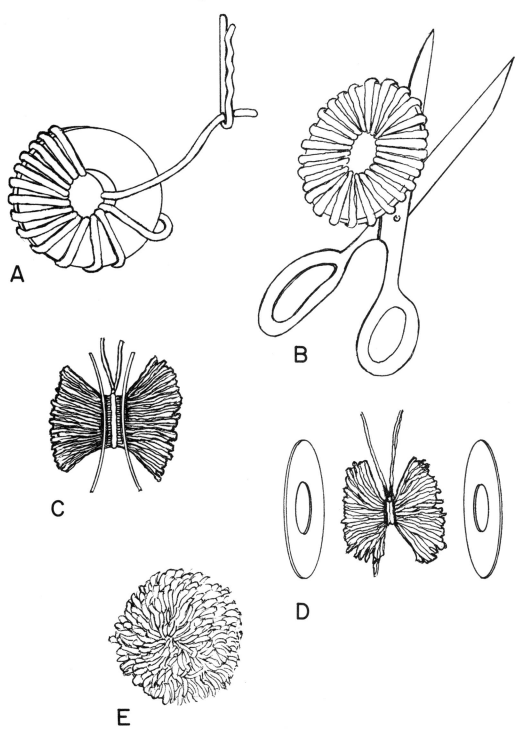

Fig. 4–11 Making a pompom. A: Wrapping yarn. B: Cutting between washers. C: Tying the yarn. D: Removing the washers and fluffing yarn. E: Finished pompom.

Figure 1 Traditional corn husk dolls are an all-time favorite. Shown here are a pilgrim, a cossack and a peasant girl.

Figure 2   Clothespin characters can be as simple as a
painted toy soldier or as elaborate as the gowned lady.

Figure 3   The lady has a cork head, the farmer and his beard are a mango seed and pine
cones make terrific novelty dolls—a cuddly baby or a strange looking bird.

washers and tie it firmly, then pull the washers off (Fig. 4–11D). Fluff up the yarn a bit, trim any wild hairs and the pompom is finished (Fig. 4–11E).

BOWS AND SUCH

A few of the things you can do with ribbons are illustrated in Figure 4–12 and some of the finished products are shown in Figure 4–10. None of them

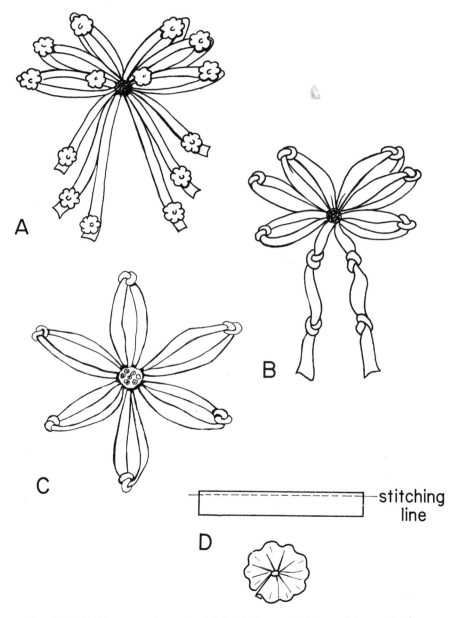

Fig. 4–12 Ribbon creations. A: Multiple bows. B: Knotted bows. C: Six-pointed star. D: Ribbon rosette.

require anything more than a few lengths of narrow, colorful ribbon and a few small pieces of felt. I usually use "baby ribbon," quarter-inch wide satin ribbon in a variety of colors.

To make the multiple bows in Figure 4–12A, lay a few lengths of ribbon together. Treating the entire bunch of ribbons as a single ribbon, tie them into a bow knot, then separate the individual bows and streamers. Sew embroidered or felt flowers—or any decorations you like—here and there on the bows and at the ends of the streamers. For felt flowers, just cut small flower shapes from felt of contrasting colors. If the ribbons are all white, multiple bows like these look pretty on bridal and baby doll dresses. In bright colors, they go especially well with European folk costumes.

To make the knotted bows shown in Figure 4–12B, tie knots at regular intervals in a two-yard length of ribbon. Form the ribbon into three long loops with a knot at *each* end of each loop. Then, treating the group of loops as a single length of ribbon, tie them into a knot at the center. Leave the ends of the ribbon dangling.

To make the six-pointed star (Fig. 4–12C), simply make the knotted bows as described in the last paragraph, then cut off the long ends. When fastening the star to fabric, arrange the loops evenly and stitch them all in place. If you want to get elaborate, you can add a few French knots (a bumpy knot used in embroidery) to the center, which makes the whole thing look more like a flower than a star.

The last item, the rosette, is made from about a foot of half-inch-wide ribbon. Run a gathering thread along one side, as indicated in the sketch at the top of Figure 4–12D, then gather the ribbon as tightly as you can. Tie the gathering thread into a tight knot. To strengthen it a bit, take a few stitches in the center of the rosette. Several such rosettes, made in different pastel colors and sewed to a piece of leafy-green ribbon, make an elegant trim. Or you could sew these onto multiple bows in place of the felt flowers if you like.

Chapter 5

Plain
and
Fancy
Clothespin
Clan

The dolls shown in the color insert, Figure 2, show the extremes you can go to with clothespins. The two small ones are little more than painted clothespins, while the other uses the clothespin only for the basic body frame.

Plain Folks

The simple ones are certainly easy to make and, if my own experience is any example, very popular—particularly among small boys who like to play with toy soldiers but who can't talk their parents into investing in the commercial variety. My younger brother, for instance, used to make soldiers like this by the battalion. The only problem was that he would always lose his army on wash day and he was never quite able to get used to the idea of his soldiers doing anything so common as holding up a line full of clothes.

PAINTING

Even with a doll as simple as the soldier there are a few precautions. First, let me say once again that if you're going to give any of these to children or let children make them themselves, be sure to use nontoxic paint. Acrylics are not only safe but can be washed off brushes, hands and faces with soap and water. For very small children it might be a good idea, also, to omit the pompom and simply paint some hair on top of the head.

As for the painting itself, there is little to say. Paint the bottom half one color and the top half, except for the knob, another color. You can either paint a face directly on the wooden knob or give the knob a coat of some appropriate color first and then paint the face on over that. If you want a sharp division between the colors, cover the part you're not painting with masking tape. That way, shaky hands won't give you any trouble. By using different colors, or adding criss-cross "straps" across the chest, you can make all kinds of uniforms.

As for the other painted clothespin, that is just to show that you can do more with clothespins than make soldiers and hang up clothes.

Fancy Clothespin Lady

Materials

For the elaborate clothespin doll shown in color (Fig. 2), you will need the following materials, in addition to a clothespin.

a cotton ball (a regular commercial size will do. You might be able to make do with the cotton from a pill bottle)

2 white pipe cleaners for arms

about 100 inches of black or brown yarn or embroidery thread for hair

about 20 inches of colored ribbon, a $\frac{1}{4}''$ wide or less

a circle of light-colored felt, 3 inches in diameter, for the hat

$3'' \times 1\frac{1}{2}''$ piece of dark felt for the purse

$3'' \times 12''$ length of plain white fabric for the head and the apron

$7'' \times 9''$ piece of colorful print fabric for the blouse and skirt

ASSEMBLY

Cut all items according to the pattern in Figure 5–1. See Chapter 2 for instructions on enlarging patterns and cutting material.

Head. Glue the cotton ball to the top of the clothespin and then force the cotton down around the knob of the clothespin. This cotton, with the knob as a central core, will form the head. Now put a small amount of glue around the bottom of the knob and around the bottom of the cotton itself and then place

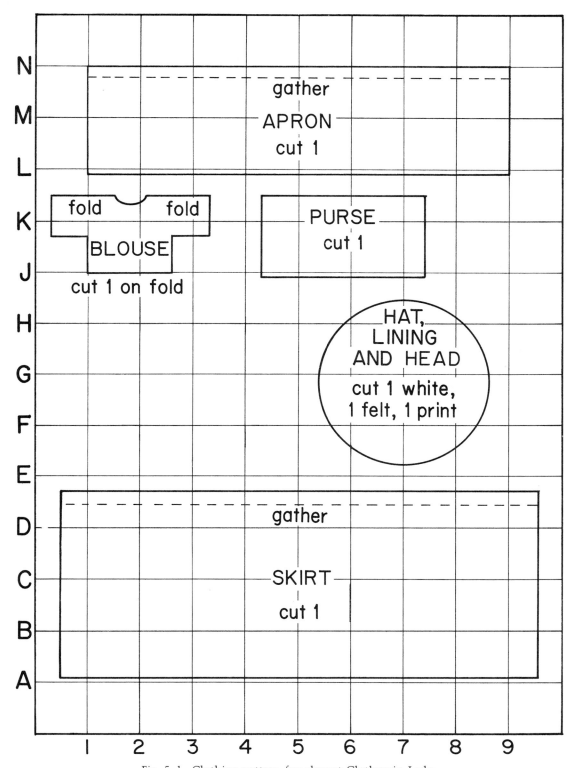

Fig. 5–1 Clothing pattern for elegant Clothespin Lady.

the fabric head piece over the cotton. Pull the cloth of the head down over the cotton, rather tightly, and squeeze it together on the glued area at the bottom. To hold the material in place while the glue dries, tie a piece of thread tightly around the bottom of the cloth. This thread can be removed once the glue has dried.

Arms. Twist the ends of two pipe cleaners together to form a single, long pipe cleaner. Wrap the double-length cleaner around the clothespin at the neck, being sure to make both arms equal length. To form hands, bend the ends of the cleaner back on themselves to form narrow loops.

Face and Hair. This is a good time to draw the face onto the fabric with a fine-pointed ink marker. If you want to add a little color to her cheeks, rub a cotton swab lightly over some lipstick and then brush the swab over the face. Be careful not to get small, solid particles of lipstick caught in the swab when you're rubbing it on the lipstick. Such particles would give the face a streaky look instead of a light, even color.

Hair, too, can be added now. Use yarn or embroidery thread to make a small skein wig of whatever style you want. For a doll this size, two-inch-long hair would be about right, so the skein you wind should be about four inches long.

Blouse. To give the blouse a more finished look, start by hemming the ends of the sleeves. The rest of the blouse needn't be hemmed because both the top and the bottom edges will be covered.

Next, fold the blouse along the shoulder line and stitch each set of arm and side seams. Put the blouse on the doll and sew up the back opening. Finally, sew a bit of rickrack or other decoration around the neckline.

Skirt. Hem the skirt across the bottom edge and then sew up the back seam. Next, run a gathering thread completely around the top of the skirt and pull the thread up fairly tightly, but not so tightly you won't have room to get the clothespin inside.

Place the skirt on the doll, tucking the bottom of the blouse inside, and pull the gathering thread up to make a snug fit. Tie the gathering thread and take a few stitches into the skirt. Finally, add a couple of stitches to fasten the skirt to the blouse.

Apron. Hem the apron on the sides and bottom. Run a gathering thread along the unhemmed edge and pull the thread up, then stitch the gathered edge in place over the skirt and blouse.

Finally, wrap some of the ribbon around the waist over the gathers of the skirt and apron. If the ribbon is too narrow to cover the tops of the skirt and apron properly, use a strip of felt that matches the purse. Another possibility, instead of felt or ribbon, would be a piece of rickrack. Whatever you use for the waistband, sew it completely across the top of the apron and then sew the ends together at the back.

stitch
here

Fig. 5–2 Hemming the bonnet ribbon.

Hat. Place the circle of print material and the felt circle together, with the *wrong* side of the print material facing up. Sew the two pieces together around the perimeter, but leave enough of an opening to turn it inside out. After turning it inside out, sew the opening closed, keeping the stitches as neat and invisible as possible.

Fold over and hem one end of a 6-inch length of ribbon as shown in Figure 5–2. Stitch this to the print side (outside) of the hat, but keep the folded-over end on the bottom, against the hat. Repeat this with another 6-inch length of ribbon on the opposite edge of the hat. Attaching the ribbons so that the edge of the hat which was stitched last is at the bottom in back, is helpful but not essential, especially if you kept the stitching neat.

Place the hat on the head, print side up, and tie the ribbons in a bow, pulling the sides of the hat down around the head. If the bow doesn't hold or if it tends to twist around and cover the doll's face, you can use a spot of glue to hold the bow in position.

Purse. Fold the rectangle of felt in the middle to form a square and sew the sides together with matching thread and an overcast stitch. For a carrying strap, sew a piece of ribbon about $1\frac{1}{2}$ inches long to the top corners of the purse. If you want to hide the ribbon stitches, sew the ribbons to the corners of the felt, inside the purse, before sewing up the sides.

Almost anything can be used to decorate the purse. I used a small piece of rickrack to match the piece at the neckline. If you do use rickrack, it works best to form it into a design before stitching it to the purse.

Since the arms are pipe cleaners, they are easy to position so they will hold the purse. Also, if the skirt is stiff enough, this doll will stand by itself.

Chapter 6

Corn Husk Beauties and Oddities

In case you've never seen one before, the animal in Figure 6–1 is a corn husk wombat. And in case you're wondering why anyone would make a corn husk wombat, I can only say, why not? I've been attracted to the animal ever since reading Will Cuppy's *How to Attract the Wombat* (Dover, 1949). Not that I would want one for a pet; they're tailless Australian rodents that weigh up to 75 pounds and, according to Cuppy, dig holes in practically anything that isn't covered with concrete. The name alone, however, is enough to make it one of my favorite animals and when I saw a postage stamp with a wombat on it, I couldn't resist using it for a model. This way I can have my wombat and not lose my back yard.

It didn't come out too badly for the first wombat I ever made, if I do say so myself. I can't help it if most people think it's a pig. (*Ridiculous!* Can't they see it has the distinctive, rounded nose of a wombat? Besides, who ever heard of a pig without a tail?)

Fig. 6–1   Pioneer girl and wombat are made by wrapping layers of corn husk around a body structure of corn stalks (wombat) or wire armature (girl).

All of which is my way of saying, "Welcome to the world of corn husks." It also goes to show that you can make more out of corn husks than pioneer women with brooms in their hands. Not that I have anything against pioneer women, with or without brooms; in fact, the girl with the hoop next to the wombat is a pioneer girl of sorts. The point is, you can make about anything you want and none of it is really very hard. Before we start making either pioneers or wombats, though, there are a few things that should be said about corn husks themselves and related items.

Obtaining and Rejuvenating Corn Husks

In the fall, most Farmers' Markets and a few groceries sell corn husks and stalks fairly cheaply, so it's best if you lay in a good supply when you can. If you run out sometime when husks are out of season, you'll have to pay the relatively high prices that arts and crafts stores charge for their small packages of husks. In addition, the packages contain nothing but husks, and you will be needing more than just husks for most of the dolls in this chapter. In fact, you'll need everything but the corn itself: husks, stalks, corn silk and corn flowers (those seedy looking tassels at the very top of the stalk).

Dry the husks until they're a nice yellowish brown. Then, to make dry husks flexible and soft again, simply soak them for a few minutes in a bucket of water. If you want them to get extra soft, add a couple teaspoons of glycerine to the water. If you're going to paint the dolls, though, the glycerine will slow you up a little: you will have to wait a little longer before the paint will stick properly. In either case, the husks will stay flexible enough to work with for only a few hours, so unless you're a fast worker, there's no point in softening more than a few husks at a time.

CORN SILK

If the corn silk is still moist when you get it, spread it out on an old newspaper and let it dry in the open air for a few days. Don't put it in any container until it is thoroughly dry; its own moisture is enough to make it mold. Once it has dried completely, you can store it in anything.

Corn Stalk Dolls

STALK MAN

Let's start with the simplest dolls, which aren't even corn husks, but corn stalks instead. Two of these are shown in Figure 6–2. The man is simplicity

Fig. 6–2 Corn stalk horse and man are the easiest figures to make: simply join sections of stalk with toothpicks.

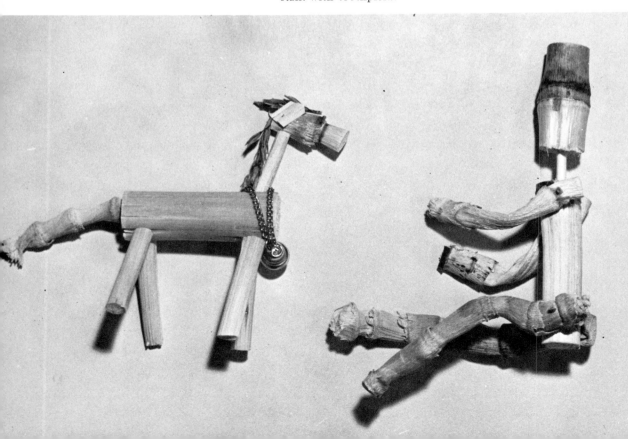

itself. Once you find some suitable pieces of stalk, put them together with a couple of toothpicks as shown in Figure 6–3. Start with the neck, which is a very narrow piece of stalk forced down into the soft center of the torso stalk. Then anchor the arms and neck by forcing a toothpick through both arms, the torso and the bottom of the neck stalk. Attach the legs the same way and then push the top of the neck stalk into the center of a large, jointed stalk used for the head.

And that's it. The stalks are soft enough to allow toothpicks to be driven through them in any direction and the centers of the large ones are soft enough to let you drive the small stalks into them.

STALK(ING) HORSE

The horse in Figure 6–2 is just as simple. The legs, neck and tail are all held on by toothpicks that are pushed deep into their centers and into the body stalk, as shown in Figure 6–4. Because the neck stalk is fairly short, the toothpick in it sticks out both ends and attaches the neck to both the head and the body. The blinders are a couple of pieces cut from the outside of a stalk and pinned to the head by straight pins. The mane, also pinned onto the head and neck, is a corn flower.

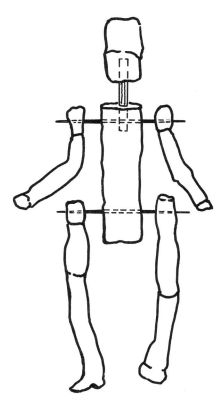

Fig. 6–3 Assembling pieces of stalk with toothpicks to form a man's body.

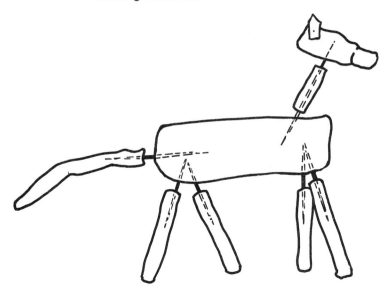

Fig. 6-4   Assembling pieces of stalk to form a horse's body
and joining with toothpicks.

Wrapped Corn Stalk Figures

WOMBAT

From the horse in Figure 6-2 to the wombat in Figure 6-1 is a short step. The skeleton is the same, except the wombat's head is bigger and is fastened directly to the front of the body by a toothpick. Before fastening the stalks together, wrap them in corn husks.

To wrap the legs and body, start by splitting several husks into strips about a half inch wide. Once you have enough strips, just start wrapping, roughly the same way you wrap a wire body with strips of stocking (Ch. 3). The only difference is, the husk strips are shorter and not as stretchy. With a little care and an occasional straight pin, the wrapping isn't hard.

Roll the head up in a single, wide piece of husk and fasten the husk in place. Gather the nose end together, put a small circle of dark felt over it, then fasten the felt and the gathered nose husk in place with two or three pins. Gather the neck end of the husk together and fasten it in place with string or a wire. Wrap another narrow husk around the neck like a collar to hide the wire or string, and pin it into place.

Once all the wrapping is complete, fasten the parts together with toothpicks.

HORSE

The best way to make the horse in Figure 6-5 is the same way the wombat was made. That is, wrap all the individual stalks in husks and then fasten them

Fig. 6–5   Corn silk hair and mane are the only adornments needed for lifelike detail on these husk-wrapped bodies.

all together with toothpicks. As you can see in the color photograph, Figure 11, the mane and tail are corn silk that has been pinned on and the ears are a couple of pieces of husk pinned to the head. The load is a milkweed pod and a batch of corn flowers tied on with a thin strip of husk. The reins are just another narrow strip of husk. The main difference between this and the wombat is in the wrapping of the legs, neck and head. Instead of wrapping several narrow strips around and around them, a couple of wider husks are wrapped around them lengthwise, as shown in Figure 6–6.

Fig. 6–6   Wrapping corn husks lengthwise around wire body structure.

Husk-Wrapped Wire Dolls

FARMER BOY

The farmer in Figure 6–5, also shown in color in Figure 11 with his horse, is a wire body wrapped in corn husks. To make it, you simply make a bare wire body as described in Chapter 3, then you wrap it with strips of corn husk instead of strips of nylon. As with the wombat, you use half-inch strips of husk for wrapping.

To make the farmer boy's head, wrap something light (like a styrofoam egg or a ball of cotton) in a corn husk and tie off the neck end with a narrow strip of husk. The head can be either pinned to the body or fastened by a wire. The hands are simply husks looped over the ends of the arm wires and held in place by the arm wrappings.

The trousers are applied with black paint and the hat is a piece of husk pinned to the top of the head. The torso is covered by a pair of husks, one over each shoulder. The bottoms are held in place at the waist by another husk, painted black and wrapped around the waist like a cummerbund, then pinned in place at the back. He is carrying an armload of corn flowers. If you prefer, you could make fabric clothing for any of these dolls, but they are much more authentic dressed with husk.

As long as the husks are still damp, you can position a husk-wrapped wire body any way you want. Once the husks are dry, however, they become quite brittle and it's safest not to disturb them.

Traditional All-Husk Dolls

PILGRIM AND PEASANT GIRL

The most traditional and folksiest of the corn husk dolls are those made entirely of husk. The girl with the flower basket in Figure 6–7, also shown in color Figure 13 with the pilgrim, are both examples of the all-husk doll. How to make the body for the all-husk doll is described in the following paragraphs.

BODY ASSEMBLY

Head. Start by rolling several pieces of husk into a ball about the size you want the head to be. This won't hold together by itself, so place the ball in the center of the widest, sturdiest husk you have. It should be at least as wide as the ball is, preferably quite a bit wider. With the ball lying in the center of the husk, pull the two ends of the husk up like the ends of a hammock and fold them over the ball. Stretch the husk around the ball as tightly as you can without tearing it and tie it in place with a piece of string around its "neck." The ends of the husk should hang down below the neck, in both front and back, at least an inch, preferably two or three.

Arms and Legs. Arms and legs are made the same way. The only differ-

Fig. 6–7   A traditional all-husk peasant girl.

ence between the two is that you might want to use thicker, longer husks for the legs. For each arm or leg, roll up three separate husks so that you have three lengths of corn husk "rope." Tie the three rolled husks together at the larger end (if the husks you're using have larger ends) with a piece of string, as shown at left in Figure 6–8.

Braid the three husks together and, when the braiding is complete, tie the

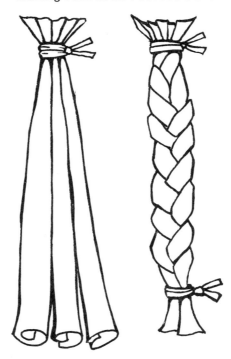

Fig. 6–8 Braiding corn husks for arms
and legs.

other ends together. It should now look roughly like the example on the right in Figure 6–8. If you want thicker arms or legs, roll two or three husks together for each "rope" instead of a single husk. Be careful with the relative size of the ropes: if one is substantially larger around than the other two, you will have trouble making the limb straight.

Assemble the arms and legs as shown in Figure 6–9. The large ends should go together, leaving the smaller ends for hands and feet. Let the limbs overlap each other a little and sew them together with four or five rough stitches. Be sure the stitches go completely through all of the husks in both limbs. It's not very practical to tie the limbs together with string because the husks will dry and shrink and the arms and legs would probably fall apart after a few days.

Assembling the Parts. First, place the arms directly beneath the neck of the head husk, between the two ends of the husk that hang down from the neck tie. To hold the arms in place, tie the neck husks together as close under the arms as you can (Fig. 6–10). If you want to be on the safe side, you can also run two or three stitches through the neck husks and the arms.

Next, lay a single husk flat on a table and place the head and arms section and legs on the husk as shown in Figure 6–10. If you want to add some body to the body, fill out the area between the arms and the legs with a few husks rolled into a ball as illustrated (the ball may have to be tied together with a string). If you don't want the body to be that long, you can move the legs up

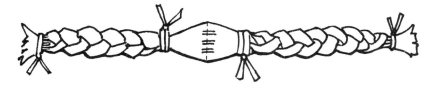

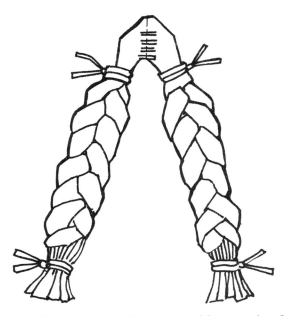

Fig. 6–9 Stitching braided arms and legs together firmly.

closer to the arms. In either event, tie the top of the large, flat husk to the bottom of the head and arms section with a string, where shown.

Now pull the lower end of the large, flat husk between the legs like a long diaper and fold it over the front of the body until it can be tied in place just beneath the arms and again at waist level. Now add a few stitches through the body and legs just to be sure everything stays put. If the single husk holding the legs on seems a little flimsy, you can add another husk in the same way the first was attached.

CLOTHES

Dress. If you're lucky, the doll now has a vaguely human shape and you can start attaching some clothes. The easiest type to make, particularly for relatively small dolls, are long dresses such as the one the peasant girl in color Figure 13 is wearing. Find a long, wide husk and slit it a short distance down the middle for a neck opening as shown in Figure 6–11. Place it over the head, down onto the shoulders, sort of like a poncho. If a single husk isn't long enough to reach all the way, use two husks; slit each husk near the end and

Fig. 6–10   Attaching braided limbs to the head and torso.

use one for the front and the other for the back, stitching them together at the shoulder. Whichever you do, tie the dress in at the waist with a narrow strip of husk.

Pants and Shirt. For pants or skirts that are separate from the shirts, hang a number of husks of the proper length from the waist and tie them with string. The only difference between skirts and trousers is that, to make

Fig. 6-11   Cutting a length of husk to make a shirt
or dress.

trousers, you tie the bottoms of the husks around the individual legs, while to
make skirts, you let them hang free.

To go with the pants, make a simple blouse or shirt the same way you
made the dress: just cut the husks off below waist level instead of letting them
go all the way to the feet.

To make bloused sleeves such as the cossack and peasant girl are wearing
(see color section, Figure 1), refer to Figure 6-12. Cut a rectangular piece of
husk at least 4 inches wide and tie it to the arm an inch or so above the point
at which you wish the end of the sleeve to be, as shown in the top sketch.
Carefully pull the husk inside out, then back over the place where it is tied to
the arm, as illustrated in the lower sketch. Tie the pulled-back end at the top
of the arm and you have your bloused sleeve.

Accessories. The bonnets on the women are just differently shaped pieces
of husk wrapped around the head and either tied or pinned in place. To make

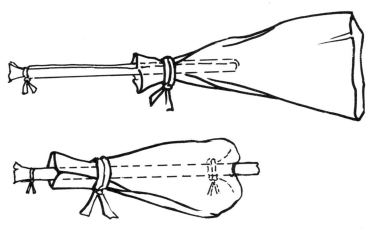

Fig. 6-12   Two steps in making bloused sleeves from a piece of
corn husk.

Fig. 6–13 Fashioning a pilgrim's collar from corn husk.

a pilgrim hat (shown in color in Figs. 1 and 13), cut a circle of husk for the brim, put a loose ball of husk on top of it in the center, then wrap a husk horizontally around the ball. The pieces of the hat are held together by straight pins here and there. The pilgrim's collar is a piece of husk wrapped around his shoulders like a cape and tied together in the front by a narrow strip of husk run through two holes in the collar husk, as shown in Figure 6–13.

DRYING and FINISHING

Before painting a face or fastening hair on the doll, it must be dried for at least a day or two, preferably longer. Since the husks are flexible until they dry, you don't want to simply prop the doll up or lay it down on something to dry. If you do, chances are that it will warp out of shape under its own weight. After it has dried, of course, the warp will remain.

To avoid this warping, I usually tie a string loosely around the body under the arms and hang it from a light fixture. Just be sure it is hanging free in the air and is not close to any heat source. Hanging it close to direct heat will make it dry faster, but it will also make the husks curl badly. Also, don't hang the doll by the neck. Aside from looking a bit macabre, this may loosen the neck and cause it to wobble.

As the doll dries, the husks shrink, so it is a good idea to check it every day and tighten any of the husks or strings that start feeling loose, particularly the waist—or belt—husks.

When drying is complete, the features can be painted on and clothes colored if you wish. The corn silk hair can also be added: just put some glue on the head and lay the corn silk over it, pushing it around until you get a style you're satisfied with.

Almost-All-Husk Bodies

This body is made exactly like the all-husk body, except that the arms and legs are not braided. Instead, each is made by wrapping a husk or two length-

Fig. 6–14 Cross section of a harvest wreath
made on a ring base from husks.

wise around a wire and tying with a string or a narrow strip of husk (*see* Fig.
6–6). The body is assembled in the same way as the all-husk body was.

Harvest Wreath

A wreath isn't really a doll, but it complements the scene shown in the
color section (Fig. 1) and you can make one very quickly. It may give you ideas
for using the same materials you used for several dolls to make accents for
grouping the dolls into a scene.

You will need a ring 5 or 6 inches in diameter: the one shown is a
Styrofoam ring, but you could fashion one out of coat hanger wire if you wish.
The husks are simply a series of overlapping bloused sleeves (*see* Fig. 6–12).
After fastening each husk with string or wire, just be sure the next husk covers
the attachment—as shown in the cross section of the wreath (Fig. 6–14).

Chapter 7

Nut
and
Seed
Family

Nut dolls are the most fun of all to make, with the possible exception of dried fruits. Not only are they easy to make, but they come in a tremendous variety of shapes, sizes and finishes, as you can see if you take a look at the relatively limited assortment in Figure 7–1.

Working with Nuts and Seeds

An easy way to get started is to buy a pound of mixed nuts from a grocery: be sure to get the kind that are still in their shells. With the right kind of nuts and a little imagination, you could make a whole village full of people from a pound of nuts. Hazel nuts or filberts, for instance, make good "winter" characters; the flat stem end can be painted as a face, while the rest of the nut

62

Fig. 7–1 An assortment of nuts mounted on pipe cleaners. The type of nut you use for the head will suggest a character.

usually looks like a hood of some kind. Fasten a couple of Brazil nuts together, like the two in Figure 7–1, and they might look like a duck. Pecans, because they are so smooth and so varied in shade, can be used for almost any type of person with appropriate features painted on.

Peanuts are probably the most versatile; they can be made into a remarkable variety of things. They can be used for heads or for complete bodies. With a felt-tip ink marker, a few pipe cleaner stubs, a little crepe paper and a few other odds and ends, you'd be surprised at what you can come up with. A few examples are shown in Figures 7–2 and 7–3. As you can see from the miniature sea lion, there's no need to limit yourself to human forms. Just make the nuts into whatever you think they resemble. As for attaching pipe cleaners, the peanut shell is thin enough to allow you (if you're careful) to poke the pipe cleaners directly into the shell. If the cleaners don't hold well enough, you can always add a drop of glue. And if you break the shell or make something you don't like, you can always eat your mistakes. Peanut creations make great party favors, too. They're easy to make, inexpensive, and can be dressed up to look like almost anything.

If you don't want to limit yourself to what you find in the store, you can always go out looking under trees in the fall—as long as you don't mind a reputation as the neighborhood eccentric. It won't be too bad, though, if you

Fig. 7–2 A bunch of peanut novelties.

can keep yourself from breaking into fits of laughter every time you find a nut that, from a certain angle, looks like one of your neighbors. As for me, I tend to chuckle a lot while I'm out there pawing through the fallen leaves and filling my sack with goodies.

The traditional nuts used for doll heads are hickory nuts and acorns. I rather like acorns myself, for a couple of reasons: like the peanut, the shell is thin and very easy to poke holes in; also, they have a natural cap and are easy to paint faces on.

There are a number of varieties of acorns; the kind I have are from the white, red and burr oak trees. The burr oak acorn usually works best if it's made into a child, while the other varieties are more dignified looking. A few simple examples (none particularly dignified) are shown in Figures 7–4 and 7–5.

In addition to the standard nuts, there are some seeds which make excellent dolls and are sufficiently nutlike to be included in this chapter. Pine

Fig. 7–3 An all-peanut sailor and his part-peanut bride.

Fig. 7–4 Acorns are one of the easiest and most versatile nuts to use.

Fig. 7–5 Dolls with acorn heads and pipe cleaner bodies can be costumed—or simply add a cane or other accessory to complete them.

cones, for instance, make good bodies for birds or harpies or other weird creatures, such as the one shown in the color section, Figure 3. The overlapping scales of the pine cone are perfect for feathers or for monsters; you can get some pretty effective creatures just by adding eyes and feet and maybe a stringy tentacle or two.

Another weird but fantastically useful seed is the mango seed, which I used to make the farmer shown in the color section, Figure 3. Actually, after I made this one, I decided it was a mistake. With a hairy face like that, I should have dressed him as a werewolf.

PREPARATION AND PRESERVATION

Nuts don't normally need any special care or preservation, other than drying. Most of the nuts you buy in a store, in fact, will already be dried, but those you pick up in a field will have to sit in a dry place for a month or so before you can use them. The only problem I've had is with acorns, which often have tiny holes in them. They may not be worm holes, but they look enough like them for me to always dry the acorns in tightly sealed bags.

Some seeds, though, will have to be cleaned pretty thoroughly before you can dry them. Peach pits can simply be scrubbed and dried with a towel. Mango seeds, however, are another matter altogether. Mangoes are very pulpy and messy. You can, if you like the taste, eat most of the mango pulp off the seed, but you have to be careful as you get near the seed. It has long, stringy hair all over it and it is virtually impossible to get all the pulp off by eating. (In fact, if I'd seen the seed first, I'm not sure I would have eaten the thing at all.) After most of the mango pulp is off the seed, wash it thoroughly and repeatedly with soap and water. Just keep washing and rinsing over and over until all the hair looks clean. Finally, to dry the seed, put it between two layers of paper toweling in a warm, dry place for a few days. (I'm not sure what the paper towels do, but the only time I tried to dry a seed without them, it changed color. Maybe wet mango seed hair is sensitive to light.) Once the seed is completely dry, use a stiff brush to fluff out the hair. Just keep brushing until the seed looks like a grizzled old man (or a grizzled werewolf, depending on what sort of imagination you have).

The main problem with mango seeds is finding one the right size. Most are horrendously large. Still, if you or some of your friends like mangoes, you're sure to eventually run across a few that are doll sized.

MOUNTING NUT HEADS

For most nut dolls, a light wire armature body is usually all that is needed. Some of the smaller ones, such as acorns, filberts and almonds, can be put on pipe cleaner bodies.

No matter what you make of a nut or seed, it will require a hole or two for mounting on a body. How you make the holes depends on the kind of nut. As I mentioned earlier, peanuts are thin-shelled enough to allow you to stick the pipe cleaners in directly, making the hole as you make the doll. Acorns are almost as easy. Use a darning needle to poke holes in them, twisting the needle a bit as you force it in.

For medium hard items, like almonds or peach pits, use something hard and sharp, like an ice pick—if you're careful. I have to admit, however, that it is much easier if you use a small electric hobby drill and hold the nut in a small vise. The shells are so thin on most nuts that you have to work carefully and slowly to avoid drilling clear through the nut.

Black walnuts are a problem for two reasons. First, they are terrifically hard, so it is almost impossible to get a hole into one without some kind of drill. And even with an electric drill, you have to be careful; I've broken more than one drill bit on black walnuts. The second problem is that the hulls of black walnuts are extremely messy and the stains you get from them are permanent. The stains will eventually wash off your hands, but they'll never wash out of clothes. (For this reason, they were once used to make brown dye.) Also, the fact that the hulls are very hard to remove add to the chances that you will stain something. Your best bet is to wear gloves and apron when you peel them.

Hickory Nut Knitter

A number of completed nut dolls are shown in the color section, Figure 5. The following instructions tell you how to make the "knitting lady," also shown in Figure 7–6.

Fig. 7–6 The Hickory Nut Knitter: an elaborately dressed nut head doll.

Materials

To make the hickory knitter, you will need a hickory nut mounted on a wrapped wire body about 5½ inches long (see Ch. 3), a little paint for the face and the following pieces of fabric.

4″ x 21″ piece of white cotton, for slip, pantalettes and apron
4″ x 16″ piece of cotton print for dress top and skirt
12″ strip of white bias tape for apron ties
Lace, 15″ for trimming skirt and sleeves (optional)

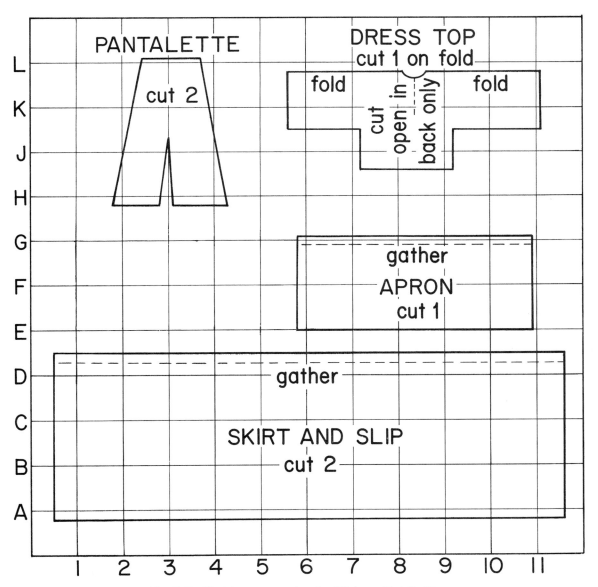

Fig. 7-7 Clothing pattern for the Hickory Nut Knitter.

ASSEMBLY

Enlarge the pattern in Figure 7–7 onto 1-inch square graph paper, lay your new pattern on the fabric and cut out all pieces.

Pantalettes. Hem the bottom of both pantalette legs and then sew the two halves together along the inseam, one side, and the bottom half of the other side. Place the pantalettes on the doll and sew the rest of the side seam so that the top of the pantalettes fit snugly around the doll's waist.

Slip and Skirt. Hem the bottom edges of both the slip and skirt. Sew up the back seams of both slip and skirt and, if desired, sew a length of lace around the bottom of the skirt for trimming.

Next, run a gathering thread around the top edge of each and fasten first the slip, then the skirt, to the doll by putting them in place and pulling in the gathering threads and tying. The skirt, slip and pantalettes can all be stitched to the body wrapping if desired, though the gathering thread should hold them in place well enough.

Dress Top. Hem the sleeve edges, then fold the dress top along the shoulder line and sew up the sleeve and side seams. Put the completed dress top on the doll. Once the garment is in place, sew up the opening in the back; overlap as much as necessary to pull the neckline in under the nut.

Apron. Hem the apron on the bottom and both sides, then run a gathering thread along the unhemmed edge. Gather the top of the apron so that it is just wide enough to reach about three quarters of the way around the doll's waist. Sew the 12 inches of bias tape to the gathered top of the apron, centering the apron so that the ends of the bias tape will serve as apron ties of equal length. Place the apron on the doll and tie it in place with a bow. If you like, the apron can be stitched to the dress.

Accessories. The knitting needles are pieces of round toothpick with beads glued on one end; the "needles" are stitched to the hands. The material she is knitting is a tiny piece I knitted myself, but you can use a piece of old sweater or pot holder or anything that looks knitted. The buttons are decorative fabric buttons I found in one of my odds-and-ends boxes that just happened to go well with the apron.

Chapter 8

Wishbone Offspring

The best part of making wishbone dolls is obtaining the wishbones, each of which is concealed deep inside a delicious bird of one kind or another. The larger the bird, of course, the larger the wishbone and the larger the doll you can make—and the more fun you can have getting to the wishbone.

When you get right down to it, though, wishbone dolls are primarily conversation pieces. The wishbones usually make up only the legs, and, if you wanted to, you could make the same legs with a wire armature. The outward appearance of a wishbone doll, therefore, is not particularly unusual. Still, it is a more inventive and folksy thing to do with leftover wishbones than simply making wishes and throwing them away.

Working with Wishbones

A few wishbone dolls are shown in Figure 4 in the color section. The one in black with the top hat just goes to show what you can think of if you let

71

your mind wander. It's a two-wishbone magician. The arms are a second, smaller wishbone. The original idea was that the wishbone arms would make him look as if he were performing a levitation act. It didn't work out exactly the way I planned, but a lot of things don't. I don't let it discourage me, though, because having things come out differently than I planned is often half the fun. They turn out better often enough, so it more than evens out.

PREPARATION

After warding off any kids who want to make wishes, clean the wishbone as thoroughly as possible and hang it up to dry for a week or so. Anywhere in the open air will do, unless you have a dog or cat who has the mistaken impression that all bones are for chewing or eating. What you do in that case depends on how persistent the animal is. Mine, an overly friendly but not overly bright Boxer named Trina, isn't much of a problem, so I usually hang my bones from a kitchen towel rack. (I haven't lost any so far, but one partially finished doll modeling for pictures was eaten by the photographer's dog!)

After all remnants still sticking to the bone are completely dry, scrape the bone thoroughly and carefully with a paring knife. Remember that the dried bone has become very brittle, so handle it accordingly.

After scraping, wipe the wishbone with some full-strength dishwashing detergent on a damp sponge. This will pull out any grease that's left on the bone. Finally, rinse the bone under a faucet and dry it with a towel.

BODY CONSTRUCTION

For the body, you need the wishbone, three pipe cleaners, and something to make a head from.

The size of the head, of course, depends on the size of the wishbone. In any case, because of the wishbone's fragility, the head should be light—use cork, balsa wood, Styrofoam®, or even an English walnut shell. A cotton-stuffed fabric head, similar to the one made for the clothespin doll in Chapter 5, would also work.

The body is constructed of three pipe cleaners and the wishbone, as shown in Figure 8–1. The length of pipe cleaner wrapped around the waist should be wound as tightly as is practical. Just be careful not to squeeze so tightly that you crack the wishbone. The head, whatever it is, has to have a hole drilled or poked into it before it is mounted on the pipe cleaner neck. Add a drop of glue if necessary to hold the head on firmly.

Wishbone Cowboy

It's only logical to make a wishbone into a cowboy, like the one shown in Figure 8–2 and in color (Fig. 4), considering the shape of the legs a wishbone

Figure 4   A cowboy and a Spanish senorita show off their wishbone legs. The magician has a two-wishbone body.

Figure 5   Nut dolls can be as plain or as elegant as you want to make them; the type of nut used for the doll's head usually dictates the kind of character he or she will be.

Figure 6 There's no end to the unique folks and critters you can make with a little yarn and a lot of imagination.

Figure 7 This stuffed sock babydoll and the spool fellow make ideal gifts for infants and small children.

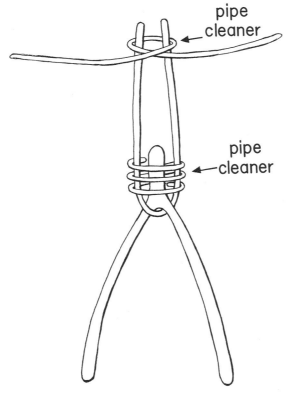

Fig. 8–1   Assembling a wishbone body with three
lengths of pipe cleaner.

gives you. Also, the tips of the wishbone sticking out of the pants legs look vaguely like cowboy boots.

Materials

Although you can use any material you wish for the clothing, I prefer felt. It is easy to sew directly onto the doll and this is what you have to do, at least to get the pants on over the wishbone legs. The material required for the wishbone cowboy's clothes, then, is just four scraps of felt in different colors, none bigger than the 4″ x 6″ piece required for the pants. You'll also want several buttons, a belt buckle and a badge.

Assembly

The pattern for the cowboy's clothing is given in Figure 8–3. Because the size of the doll, and therefore the size of the clothes, depends on the size of the wishbone, you will probably have to adjust the size of the pattern to match, even after you expand it onto a graph with 1-inch squares (see Ch. 2 for instructions on altering patterns). Since all parts of this pattern are relatively simple, adjusting it should not be much of a problem.

Fig. 8-2 The Wishbone Cowboy: a sheriff itching to get his man.

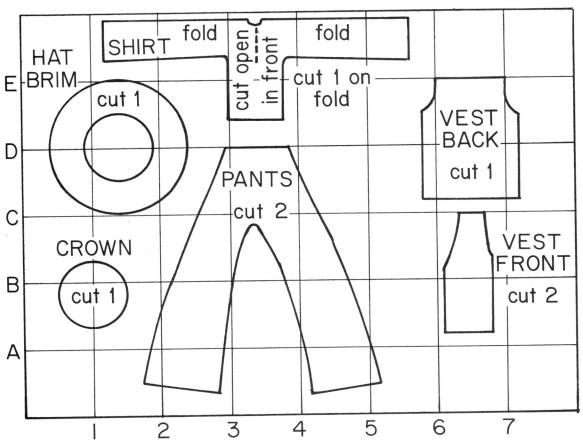

Fig. 8–3 Clothing pattern for the Wishbone Cowboy.

Shirt. Start by folding the shirt along the shoulder line and sewing up the sleeve and side seams with an overcast stitch. Place the shirt on the doll and close the front opening using a widely spaced ladder stitch.

Pants. Start on the pants by sewing the inseams, then placing them on the doll. Sew around the outer edges with an overcast stitch unless you want some fringe. To get the fringe, use a running stitch or a backstitch to sew along a line a quarter of an inch in from the edge. Then clip the material outside the line of stitching into narrow strips. The only trouble you'll encounter is that felt is difficult to sew with anything other than an overcast stitch.

Vest. Sew the two halves of the vest front to the vest back along the shoulder seams and side seams. Place the vest on the doll and close the front, bringing the right side over the left side, overlapping until the vest fits. Stitch the front pieces together and use the same thread to fasten on the three button beads.

Hat. Sew the crown onto the center of the brim using a ladder stitch.

Next, to bulge the crown up a bit, wet the crown and press it down firmly onto the doll's head or onto anything else that is round and the right size. This should stretch the felt to give it the rounded shape you want. Leave it in place until it dries. Finally, turn up the brim on the sides as shown in Figure 8–2, pin it in place and dampen the bent parts with a mixture of half white glue and half water. Once it has dried, remove the pins.

The hair is mohair, unraveled from an old sweater. It can be fastened onto the head with a bit of white glue here and there, as can the hat, once the hair has been fastened into place.

Accessories. The buttons on the vest are small beads and the badge is a star-shaped sequin. The belt and buckle are from a play watch. Make loops in the pipe cleaner for hands or glue a sunflower seed into position on each limb (Fig. 8–2).

Chapter 9

Pedigreed Gourd Group

If you've always thought of gourds as being simply "gourd shaped," you're probably in for a surprise! They come in all shapes and sizes, with many surface variations. The most common kinds, though, are rather lumpy or streaked; many look as if they have a bad case of vegetable acne, as you can see from the assortment in Figure 9–1. As a result of these gourdian imperfections, you probably won't be able to make many "pretty" dolls with gourds, but the possibilities for character or novelty dolls are endless.

Needed: A Gourd Imagination

A couple of the wilder gourds I've seen recently are shown in the accompanying photos. If you have an imagination like mine, the one in Figure 9–2 could look like either a spaceship (Buck Rogers style) or the face of someone

Fig. 9–1 A sample assortment of the varied gourds you can grow from a single package of seeds.

who just bit into a lemon. The tentacled one in Figure 9–3 makes a nice monster body, topped by a round gourd with the appropriate number of eyes painted on. Turn the same gourds upside down, as in Figure 9–4, and you have a king looking sad, probably because his crown is so lumpy.

Then there is Gourdon the gourd, shown in Figure 9–5, who is nothing more than a gourd and six pipecleaners in a cardboard coffin. As I said, the novelty possibilities are endless.

Three of my favorite "character" gourds, all based on historical characters, are shown in the color section. They just go to show how far out you can go if you really want to get carried away. They represent Henry VIII and his daughter Elizabeth I (see Fig. 12) and Kaiser Wilhelm—unrelated, so far as I know (see Fig. 10). A pattern and instructions for making the Kaiser are given at the end of this chapter.

Fig. 9–2 A spaceship? Let the shape of the gourd suggest its use.

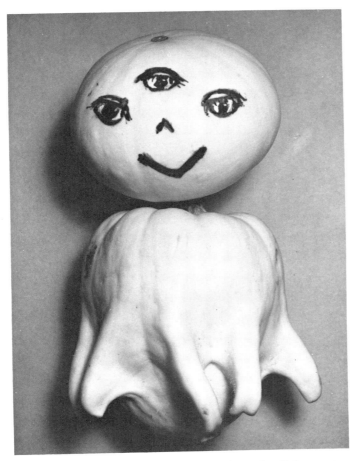

Fig. 9–3 One arrangement of two gourds: a ghoulish monster.

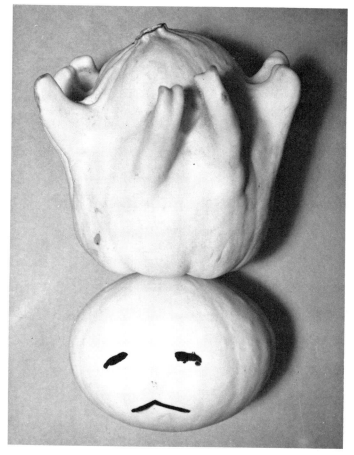

Fig. 9–4 Turn the gourds in Figure 9–3 upside down and you've got a king with a most peculiar crown.

GETTING YOUR GOURDS

You can usually find a few gourds at your local Farmers' Market, if you have one, or at roadside stands in the fall of the year. The major problem is that most of the gourds people have for sale are too large for doll heads. The growers probably throw away any that are that small. Still, you can find a few if you look.

As for me, I prefer to grow my own. A package of gourd seeds costs thirty or forty cents at a grocery store. I have never been much of a gardener, though, so I usually give my gourd seeds to my youngest child. So far I've been able to keep her believing that it's a real privilege to grow gourds not only for Autumn decorations but for Mommy's dolls. (She stopped believing in Santa Claus some time ago, so I don't know how much longer this can last.)

Even if you don't have an easily conned child, gourds for dolls' heads are

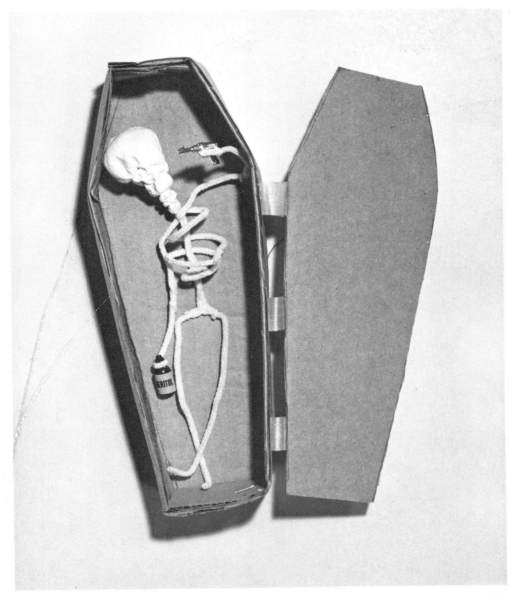

Fig. 9–5 Gourdon the Gourd: a cardboard coffin, a couple of pipe cleaners and, naturally, a gourd.

one of the easiest things to grow. Directions are on the seed packages, but if you're going to raise doll heads, you probably should ignore most of them. In the first place, plant them where they will get lots of sun and very little space. Someplace where the plants will be crowded between grass and brush is good. Also, never weed them; the weeds, like the crowding, will help keep the plants and gourds small and stunted. Just plant the seeds and forget about them until fall. Your neighbors will think you're a lousy gardener, but if you've been out in the yards and fields digging around for odd-looking nuts to make the dolls in Chapter 7, you will already have a reputation.

PREPARATION AND DRYING

Once fall comes and the vines dry up, you can pick the gourds. The drier the vines, the more likely the gourd is to be ripe. Green gourds tend to be pretty mealy inside and are even more difficult to dry properly than the ripe ones.

The first thing to do is wash the gourds. Pour a little household bleach on a rag and use that to wipe the gourds off thoroughly. The objective is not so much to get it clean as to prevent mold, which is always the prelude to rotting. This washing should be repeated every month at least, more often if the air is damp. Even so, there's no guarantee that the gourds will dry instead of rot. At least, though, you will have a better chance, say fifty–fifty. You just have to remember to start out with two or three times as many gourds as you will eventually need.

Set them in any warm, dry place and leave them alone, except for the periodic cleaning, for two or three months. I've heard of impatient people who have tried to drill small holes in the gourds to speed up the process, but the only ones I've tried it on just rotted faster and didn't dry at all. Heating them in an oven doesn't work, either; it just gives you badly cooked gourds. You can usually tell when a gourd is dry enough by shaking it. If it's dry, the seeds inside will rattle.

Once the gourd is fully dried, you can give it a little extra protection by coating it with clear shellac or varnish. Normally, if the gourd has survived the drying process without rotting, it won't need any extra protection.

PICKING A CHARACTER

Look at your gourd from all angles to see if it stimulates your imagination. Notice not only the shape, but the color and texture as well. Ask a small child what it looks like. Youngsters often see things and make associations that adults would never think of.

Take the Kaiser, for instance, shown alone in Figure 9–6. Once I had the doll made, it seemed perfectly obvious that his nose was meant to be a nose. But you'd be surprised how long I stared at it and considered using the long end for a neck instead.

THE BODY

Wire bodies are best for gourd heads. The size of the body and thickness of the wire, of course, depend on the size and weight of the gourd. Unusually

Fig. 9–6 Kaiser Wilhelm: a most distinguished gentleman with a most distinctive nose.

heavy gourds may require bodies made from coat hanger wire, while very light ones (like Gourdon) can be used on pipe cleaners.

To attach the gourd to the body, drill a hole straight through the gourd from the bottom (neck) to the top. Keep the holes just large enough for the wire you plan to use. If you don't have a drill, you can probably make do with a sharp darning needle or an ice pick.

As shown in Figure 9–7, stick a wire through the neck loop of the body, double it over, then poke the folded wire up through the holes in the gourd. To fasten the head on, thread the wires through two holes of an ordinary shirt button and twist the wires together on top of the button. You can always cover the button with hair or a hat or, if you like, you could fasten the wires to the hat itself, which is what I did with the Kaiser.

THE DRESSING

Dressing these dolls is a lot of fun. If you've decided on a specific historical character, look up a picture of the real person in an encyclopedia or

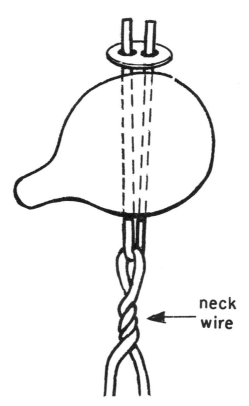

neck wire

Fig. 9–7 Attaching a gourd head to a wire armature body. Use a button to fasten the wires firmly into place.

biography and make a rough approximation of the clothes. On this type of doll, felt works well because you can sew the clothes directly on the doll. Also, with felt, there's no need to hem anything. The decorative accessories are very often more important than the clothes themselves. They give an authentic touch that will make the character identifiable. Do some digging in any boxes of junk or broken jewelry you have around the house.

In short, I like to make the clothing and accessories on gourd dolls as elegant as possible. The contrast with the head is usually so severe that the dolls are real attention getters and sometimes downright funny.

Kaiser Wilhelm

Materials

To make the Kaiser, you will need a gourd with a respectable nose, a fairly fatly wrapped wire body approximately 9 inches long (Ch. 3), and the following materials.

8″ x 13″ of dark blue felt for jacket and trousers
black vinyl or leather, 4″ x 8″, for boots
1 yard of gold braid for trim
scraps of red and black felt for mustache, mouth and trouser trim

ASSEMBLY

Cut all parts according to the pattern in Figure 9–8 after adjusting it for your particular gourd.

Trousers. Place the front and back pieces of the trousers together; sew up both the inseams and the side seams with an overcast stitch. Then sew on a strip of ¼-inch wide red felt the entire length of each side seam.

Place the assembled trousers on the doll and either take a tuck in the waist portion or pad out the body to fit. Stitch the top of the trousers to the body.

Jacket. Fold along the shoulder line and stitch the sleeve and side seams. Place the jacket on the doll, overlapping the trouser tops, and stitch the front together from the neck to about an inch from the bottom. Sew a double width of gold braid around the jacket, level with the point at which you stopped stitching. Add a buckle of some sort at the front of the belt. Stitch single strips of braid around the collar and around the sleeves at elbow level. Run a strip of braid down the outside of the sleeve from elbow to wrist. Sew a loop of braid to the belt braids to hold the sword.

Boots. Fold each boot piece in half and sew the edges together. Place the boots on the feet over the trouser legs and bend the wires to form feet.

Face and Accessories. Sketch a couple of simple cartoon eyes and ears

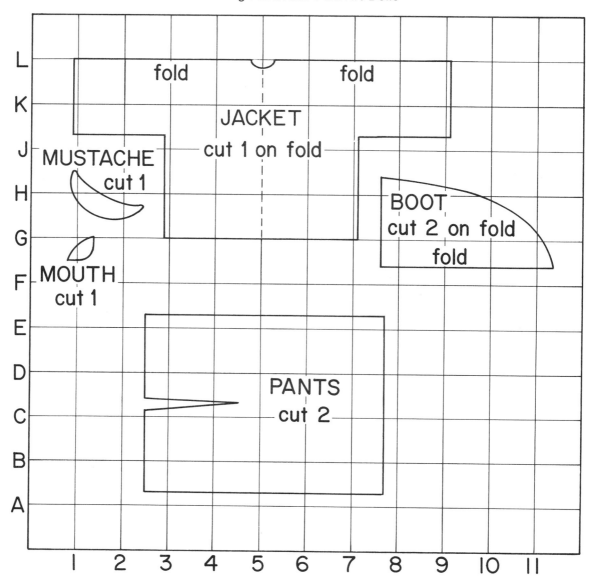

Fig. 9–8 Clothing and facial feature pattern for Kaiser Wilhelm.

until you get satisfactory results. Glue the red felt mouth to the bottom of the black felt mustache, then glue both onto the gourd underneath the nose.

The helmet I used was one I was lucky enough to find in a Red Baron race car kit, but there are lots of things you could use, including spray can lids. The sword I used started life as a pick in a mixed drink. The buttons and medals are just odds and ends—from my collection of odds and ends!

Chapter 10

Spool,
Yarn
and
Sock
Dolls

The dolls in this chapter are mostly the sort that small children can play with and, in most cases, make themselves. The only exception is the fully dressed sock doll: the doll itself can be made quite easily; it's only the dressing that takes a little time and work, and there's no need to get as elaborate as I did. Examples of spool, yarn and sock dolls are shown in the color section, Figures 6, 7, and 15.

Spool Dolls

Spool dolls, such as the one shown in color (Fig. 7) are extremely easy to make and babies less than a year old will usually have more fun with them than they will with most commercially made dolls. Empty thread spools and a few shoelaces or some heavy string are all you need. They look nice if they're painted brightly, but it's not necessary. *Just be sure the spools are all wooden,* not plastic or styrofoam of some kind. The latter can be bitten apart too easily and pieces swallowed or even inhaled. The wooden spools are quite safe as long as you remember to use nontoxic paints. The spools have already been sanded smooth, so you needn't worry about splinters. The only trouble is, it's becoming increasingly difficult to find wooden spools these days.

As for colors, bright primaries are best. To paint them, just daub acrylic paint on and put them somewhere to dry. Since both ends of the spool have to be painted, though, you can't just set them on a table or a piece of paper. You need a drying rack of some kind and the kind I use, shown in Figure 10-1, is about as inexpensive as you can get. It's just an old egg carton turned upside down with large nails stuck into each compartment.

Strange as it may seem, there are two ways of making a spool doll. One way is simply to make one string of spools for the body and head, another string for the arms and a third for the legs. Tie large knots at the end of each string to keep the spools on, then tie the strings together at body joints.

Another way is to make a shoestring skeleton first. This is something like a wire body, only it's made from shoestrings. The strings are easier to tie

Fig. 10–1   A drying rack for painted spools can be made from an egg carton and a handful of nails or pegs.

together this way, but you may have a little difficulty sliding the body spools up over the "hip" knot in the string.

Either way you do it, sort out the spools so that you use all the same size on the arms and a larger size for the legs and torso. If you want a Popeye effect, you could use large spools for the wrists and ankles, smaller ones for the upper arms and legs.

Yarn Dolls

Yarn dolls are excellent for any child old enough to not chew and suck on the yarn ends. Since the yarn is quite long, there's always a slight chance of choking. Then, too, some yarns are not colorfast and you could end up with an oddly colored child. For anyone over a couple of years old, though, they are perfectly safe and very attractive. Also, some of them can be made, literally, in a few minutes.

LOOPED YARN DOLLS

The looped yarn dolls are the easiest to make. The sequence is outlined in Figure 10–2. Start by laying out a loosely looped skein of yarn. Each of the yarn dolls in color Figure 6 is made from a single, 4-ounce skein of knitting worsted weight yarn, plus a little contrasting yarn where necessary.

First cut 7 pieces of yarn, each about 10 or 12 inches long, from the skein: these will be used as ties. Tie the first piece of yarn tightly around the skein at one end, as shown in Figure 10–2A. That tie will be the top of the head. Next, cut off the bottom one third of the skein: this should give you a batch of yarn roughly 15 to 20 inches long, which will be used for arms later.

Now hold the top two thirds of the yarn by the tie at the top and shake the yarn out, getting it as smooth as you can. Make a ball of stuffing 2 or 3 inches in diameter: wadded up cloth, cotton or anything will do. Place this stuffing into the center of the yarn, directly under the head tie. Now arrange the yarn around the stuffing so that the stuffing is completely covered and then tie one of the yarn pieces tightly around the neck.

Divide the body in two and lift the top half up and over the head, as shown in Figure 10–2B. Now tie each end of the arm section of yarn tightly and lay the arms on the body yarn as shown.

Next is an optional step, the result of which is decorative but not essential to the doll. Make a small skein of contrasting color yarn, long enough to reach from just below the arms to the bottom of the body yarn: roughly 12 inches. Cut the skein open and lay the strands of yarn across the body yarn just below the arms, as shown (Fig. 10–2B).

Bring the remaining half of the yarn down over the arms and the contrasting yarn. Leave the arms sticking straight out, but fold the contrasting yarn

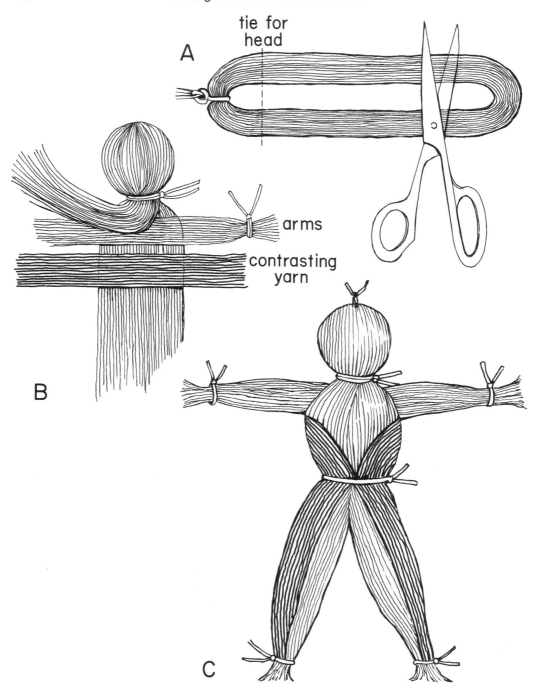

Fig. 10-2 Looped yarn doll. A: Cutting the yarn skein. B: Folding, stuffing and adding contrasting color. C: Positioning the yarn to tie waist and limbs.

down along the outside of the body yarn (Fig. 10–2C). Now tie the waist string tightly around both the body yarn and the contrasting yarn. (Stuffing can be added to the body before you tie it if you think necessary.)

Divide the yarn into legs below the waist and tie each near the bottom, at the ankles. The contrasting yarn should make up a fairly large area on the outside of each leg, as shown in Figure 10–2C and on the clown doll (see color section, Fig. 6).

The only decoration you want for this type of doll is some sort of face, and possibly a hat to cover up the knot on top of the head. Circles of felt can be glued or stitched on fairly easily, although I prefer to stitch on those plastic roll-around eyes that you can buy in most dime stores.

BRAIDED YARN DOLLS

The braided yarn doll, while simpler in some ways than the looped yarn doll, will take longer to make, simply because you have to do a lot of braiding. You start again with a 4-ounce skein of yarn and cut off seven pieces of yarn to use as ties. Then lay out the yarn and make the first tie at one end, as shown in Figure 10-3A. This knot will again be the top of the head.

Next, cut the skein of yarn open at the bottom end and place some stuffing up under the knot at the top of the head. Tie the neck tightly, then divide the rest of the yarn into three parts. Lay a quarter of it to the left for an arm and a quarter to the right for another arm: leave the rest lying straight down for the body. Tie another piece of yarn around the waist, about 4 inches down from the neck. Divide the yarn below the waist into legs. All you have to do now is braid each arm and leg, then tie them at the wrists and ankles.

As with the looped yarn dolls, plastic eyes or felt features can be sewed on easily enough. On these dolls, though, other clothes can be used if you like. The braids are thinner than the loops and lend themselves more to being dressed.

The simplest of the yarn dolls is the octopus shown in color (Fig. 15). For that, you simply make a head, tie off the neck and divide the "body yarn" into eight parts. Then braid each section separately and tie off.

Sock Dolls

Sock dolls are another easy type to make; at least, the bodies are. The three steps—from sock to dressed doll—are shown in Figure 10–4.

Materials

All you need for the body is a single child's sock and some stuffing material. For the clothes, if you want to dress it like the one in color (Fig. 7) you will need the following.

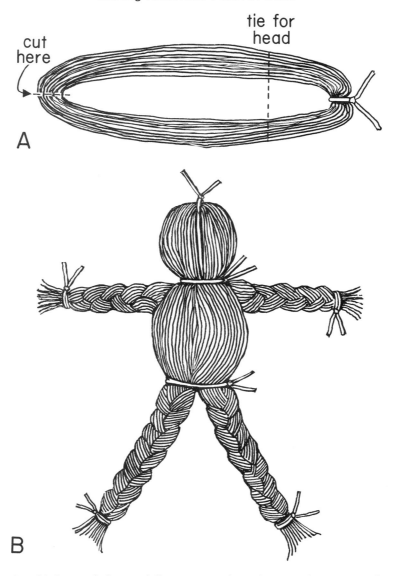

Fig. 10–3 Braided yarn doll. A: Cut and tie the yarn skein. B: Stuff
the body, fold the yarn into position and tie.

approximately ½ yard of cotton fabric of whatever colors you choose,
    for the dress and bonnet
8½″ x 3″ of nonwoven interfacing for stiffening the bonnet brim
    (thin cardboard could also be used, but then the bonnet won't be
    washable)
6″ of ¼″-wide elastic
approximately 18″ of white bias tape
yarn for hair

Fig. 10–4 Three simple steps to making a sock doll.

18″ of ½″ or narrower ribbon for bonnet strings
4 yards of rickrack in various sizes for dress and bonnet trim
    (optional)
¼ lb. stuffing material

BODY

Cut the sock into five parts as shown in Figure 10–5. Run a gathering thread around the sock about 2½ inches from the toe of the sock. Stuff this portion to form the head, then pull the gathering thread up tightly and tie. Stuff the rest of the sock to form the body and sew it closed at the bottom.

Fold each arm and leg piece in half and stitch along the curved line indicated in Figure 10–6. Turn the arm and leg pieces inside out, stuff them and sew them to the body.

Embroider or paint on a face and add some yarn hair (Ch. 4).

ASSEMBLY

Enlarge the pattern in Figure 10–7 onto 1-inch square graph paper, then cut all parts of the dress and bonnet.

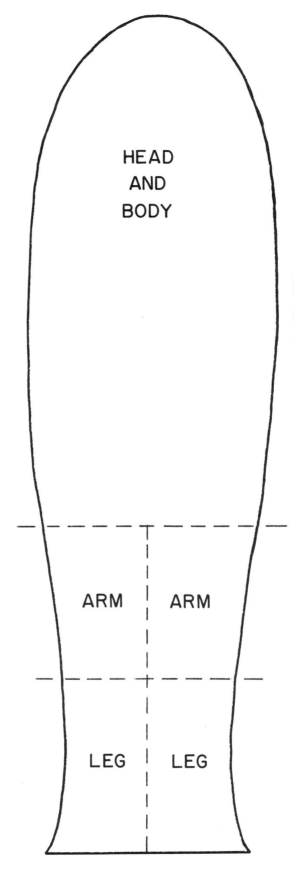

HEAD
AND
BODY

ARM | ARM

LEG | LEG

Fig. 10–5 Pattern for cutting a sock into five parts to make the babydoll.

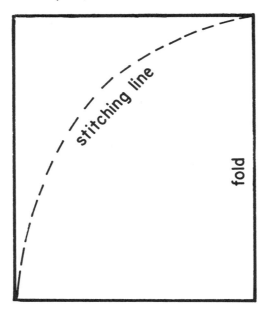

Fig. 10–6 To make arms and legs for the doll,
stitch each sock part along the line as shown.

Dress. Place the two halves of the dress top together and stitch the shoulder seams. Next, hem the bottom ends of the sleeves and stitch approximately 3 inches of elastic about ½ inch up from the hemmed end of each sleeve, *stretching* the elastic as you sew. This will form gathers when released, making puffed babydoll sleeves.

Next, run a gathering thread around the top of the sleeves and, pulling up the gathers to fit, sew the sleeves to the bodice. When the sleeves are attached to the dress top, sew up the sleeve and side seams. Turn the neck edge under and stitch it, then sew some rickrack around it.

Hem the skirt along the bottom edge, using a 1-inch hem. Sew the back seam of the skirt approximately half way up from the bottom and then bind or hem the edges the rest of the way to the top of the skirt. Sew rickrack around the bottom of the skirt as desired. I used three pieces of various sizes around mine, but that may be a bit much.

Run a gathering thread around the top of the skirt; sew the skirt to the dress top, pulling up the gathers evenly to fit smoothly to the bodice.

You can either sew up the back of the dress after it's on the doll or you can make the dress removable by sewing on small snaps.

Bonnet. Place the two pieces of the bonnet brim together, right sides on the *inside*, and place the interfacing (stiffening) on top of the two. Stitch all three together completely around the curved edge. Press and clip the curved edges, then turn the brim inside out, so that the interfacing is sandwiched

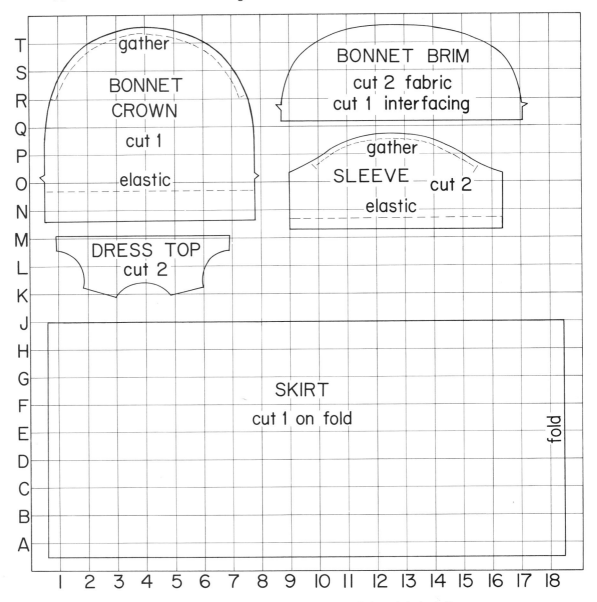

Fig. 10–7 Clothing pattern for the stuffed sock babydoll.

between the fabric pieces and the right sides of both pieces of fabric are *outside.*

Run a gathering thread along the curved edge of the crown piece of the bonnet as indicated on the pattern (Fig. 10–7) and then sew a 3-inch strip of elastic along the bottom of the crown at the level indicated by the dashed line on the pattern, *stretching* the elastic as you sew.

Sew the unfinished edge of the brim to the crown, from one end of the elastic to the other, as indicated by the tabs. Pull in the gathers in the top of the crown to fit the brim as you sew. Use bias tape to bind the exposed edges of the crown and the crown–brim seam. Finally, sew a 9-inch length of ribbon to each side of the bonnet near the ends of the elastic. These will serve as ribbon ties. If desired, add a strip of rickrack along the front of the brim on the bottom side.

Chapter 11

Carved Head Retinue

Carving, I will admit at the outset, is not my thing. It's not that I don't like to do it; I'm just not very good at it. Still, as in many other activities, I don't let a simple lack of skill stand in my way. It's fun in small doses and, as long as I stick to easily carved materials, the results aren't too terrible. Or so I tell myself. And I can always get a little help from my husband or son, who occasionally get into the act just to show me up. Three heads, one of each kind covered in this chapter, are shown in Figure 11–1 and the Uncle Sam soap head doll is also included in the color section, Figure 8.

Styrofoam Doll Heads

For the rank beginner, the best thing to start with is Styrofoam, that very light, porous plastic that is often used as packing protection. You can buy Styrofoam in variety stores in almost any basic shape—round balls, ovals, cubes, etc. It costs less than fifty cents for a head-sized piece, so it's relatively

Fig. 11–1 An assortment of dolls with hand-carved heads: from left, the lady has a head of balsa wood, Uncle Sam is a soaphead and the rather dubious looking character in the corner has a Styrofoam head.

cheap. Because it is extremely soft, all you need for carving is a sharp paring knife and a few toothpicks or lollipop sticks for poking small holes into the head.

CARVING

There are a couple of disadvantages to Styrofoam. For one thing, it splits very easily. That isn't always a total disaster, because it can be glued back together fairly easily with ordinary household cement. Another problem is the extreme porousness. Occasionally it seems like you're trying to carve a small, dry sponge, it's so full of tiny air pockets. This characteristic precludes the carving of any really delicate features, of course, but if you're like me, it doesn't really matter. If anything, it gives me an excuse for a lumpy looking carving. And the Styrofoam head at right in Figure 11–1 is certainly lumpy enough.

To avoid the splitting problem, try to keep all cuts as simple as possible and avoid making excess cuts whenever you can. If you really work at it, you can sometimes get away with no carving at all beyond what it takes to get the Styrofoam into the approximate shape of a head. Features can be made by denting the material with a stick. Or you can make an eye, for instance, by simply pushing a bead into the material. If you want to have a socket around the eye, make an indentation before you put the bead in. The end of a knife handle, your fingernails or almost anything would work, depending on the size and shape of eye socket you want.

FEATURES

Once you have the Styrofoam shaped roughly like a head, use a pencil to draw a simple face on it. It's best to make cartoon or novelty faces rather than trying for pretty ones. Large features are less likely to break off once they're carved, so don't try for small or delicate features.

If you have readymade Styrofoam balls or eggs, you can use these for heads just as they are without any carving at all. Just stick things in them. Pins with large heads, for example, can be pushed all the way into the ball, leaving only the heads sticking out for eyes or a nose. Similarly, colored thumbtacks make passable ears and a row of stickpins with the round, colored heads make a mouth of sorts. For hats, the tops of spray cans work very well. One current deodorant can, for instance, has a gold, dome-shaped cap that makes an excellent helmet.

MOUNTING

Unless you're using something very heavy for a hat or other decoration, a simple pipe-cleaner body is adequate support for a Styrofoam head. For party decorations, you can dress the figures with crepe paper clothing, which could be changed for different occasions. If you use the readymade balls with pinned and tacked-on features, they are cheap enough and easy enough to make for you to put together whole groups of them for table decorations. Or, if you're giving a party for children, you could pass out some of the balls and let them make their own faces—a sort of pin-the-face-on-the-ball game.

Soap Doll Heads

Results of soap carving are always novel and often enchanting. It is a bit harder to use than Styrofoam, however; for one thing, it splits almost as easily, but is harder to glue back together, though not impossible. You can, of course, make soap flakes out of your mistakes. That way, at least, nothing goes to waste. In fact, that is one of the reasons I use a white facial soap for most of my carving; the mistake flakes (as well as the cuttings from the carving itself) are perfect for delicate laundry.

CARVING

You proceed with soap in much the same way as with Styrofoam. First you find a piece of soap that matches the size of head you want, then you carve it into the desired oval or sphere. I usually use half of one of those large bars of Ivory®, which is about the right size for most of my soap heads. If you want to be a bit more elaborate, you could use the whole bar and carve a torso out of the lower half. In that case, carefully push and rotate a sharp darning needle through the shoulder portion, then insert a length of wire through the hole for arms. The same procedure applies to the bottom of the torso and the legs. Once you have the arms and legs in place, you could wrap them just as you do a complete wire armature body. I usually stick to just the head, but occasionally carve hands.

The first step is to draw in the features with a pencil. Once you have them drawn to your satisfaction, start cutting. A paring knife will work fairly well here, although an X-acto® knife might work better. I rarely use one, though, because they are so terribly sharp and the soap is so slippery that accidents are likely.

Because soap breaks apart fairly easily, keep your cuts small and careful. Do everything a step at a time. On the nose, for instance, cut down the sides just a short distance, then cut from the cheek to the nose until the two cuts meet. Lower the face gradually this way. *Use the tip of the knife:* it gives you better control than if you tried to use the middle of the blade.

After roughing out the facial features, you can smooth off the surfaces by holding the knife at a right angle and gently scraping over the carved portions. Just remember that the soap is soft and it won't take much of a slip for the knife to make an unexpected cut where you don't want it, either in the soap or in yourself.

SOAP HEAD WIGS

The simplest way of getting hair on a soap head is to glue on an ordinary yarn skein wig or, as for the Uncle Sam doll, some fluffed out cotton. This should be done after you have coated the head, though, which I'll talk about in the following section. For one thing, the glue sticks better to the coating; for another, coating the head after you put the wig on would give you a stiff coated wig, which wouldn't be too hot!

If you have more time and patience than you know what to do with, you might want to fasten each strand of yarn to the head individually, somewhat like the lotsa-loops yarn wig. This has to be done before coating and it helps a little if the yarn is damp (but not wet). To attach the yarn, simply lay the end of each strand on the head and push it into the soap with the eye end of a needle. Repeat this an endless number of times, being careful not to pull out old yarn strands as you push in the new: this is more likely to happen with

damp than with dry yarn. Once the soap dries it will hold better, but as long as it's damp, the yarn is fairly easy to pull out.

AGING AND PRESERVING

Whether you age a head or preserve it depends on your own taste. If you want the soap to have a yellowish tinge like old ivory, just let it stand around the house a few months or put it in an oven with a pilot light for a couple of weeks. The only problem with the oven is that, if you don't stick a note on the oven controls, someone (maybe yourself if you're as absentminded as I am) is sure to come along and turn the oven on without looking inside to see if you have some soap in there. Even notes don't help sometimes, so there's always a chance you will end up with baked soap.

On the other hand, if you want the soap head to remain the color you started with, coat the entire thing with lacquer or clear fingernail polish. Either one will keep the soap from deteriorating or changing color for several years. These coatings also give you a sheen, so if you want the old ivory look with a sheen over it, just wait until the soap has aged before you coat it.

MOUNTING

Soap heads are fairly heavy, so you will need a sturdy body. As with most heads, I prefer a wire body. You will have to make it from strong wire, perhaps a coat hanger. To mount the head, make a hole in the bottom with a darning needle. Go slowly and carefully with the needle; you wouldn't want to wreck the whole thing when it's almost done. A head has to be mounted on the body *before* it is aged; aged soap is too dry and brittle to do anything with. In fact, aged soap without a coating is so brittle it will probably shatter if dropped.

Balsa Wood Doll Heads

CARVING

Balsa is the easiest of woods to carve, but even so it is more difficult than soap. It's very soft and light, but it is also quite grainy and can easily split along those grains. It's relatively expensive, so you want to be sure you've gotten enough practice on the soap and Styrofoam to acquire a little skill before you start on balsa wood.

The carving of balsa must also be done with short, careful strokes. The main difference between it and soap is that balsa takes more strength to cut through it, so you will need sharper knives. For balsa, then, you would be better off using an X-acto knife. A paring knife, no matter how well sharpened, would not work very well. Since the wood is not as slippery as the soap, there isn't as much danger of slipping, but you still have to be very careful.

MOUNTING

Wigs, of course, have to be painted or glued on. The heads are quite light, so the body, probably a wrapped wire body, could be correspondingly light. A drop of glue will hold the head on the body once the neck wire is stuck into the hole drilled in the bottom of the head.

Uncle Sam

Materials

To make something approximating the Uncle Sam doll, you will need the carved head and hands mounted on a wrapped wire body—fairly skinny and approximately 11 inches high—and the following materials.

9″ x 18″ of blue felt for the coat
8½″ x 12″ of red and white striped material for pants
a purchased hat in the appropriate pattern
4″ x 8″ of black felt for shoes
4″ x 5″ of dark blue velvet for collar (if you don't have velvet, any
    darker blue, heavy material will do)
some cotton for hair and beard
approximately 3″ x 4″ of dark blue material for a dickey

ASSEMBLY

Enlarge the pattern in Figure 11–2 onto 1-inch graph paper and cut out all pattern parts.

Pants. Place the right and left halves of the pants together and sew front and back center seams, then hem the bottom of each leg. Turn under the waist and stitch, then sew the inseams. Place the pants on the doll and either sew in darts to make the pants fit the body or pad out the body.

Coat. Fasten the two front sections of the coat to the back half by sewing across the shoulder seams. Sew the sleeves to the coat and then sew up the sleeve and side seams.

Fold the collar material along the fold line, with right sides of the fabric *inside.* Sew the edges of the two short sides together, then turn the collar right side out. Sew the curved edge of the collar to the neck opening of the coat. The collar should be centered so that there is a ¾-inch lapel left on both ends of the collar.

Wrap a 3″ x 4″ piece of dark blue material (the shirt front) around the upper part of the body immediately below the head and stitch it to the body in the back. Now place the coat on the body and sew the two halves of the coat front together, bringing the right half over the left. Turn down the collar and lapels. The shirt front should cover all of the wrapped body that would

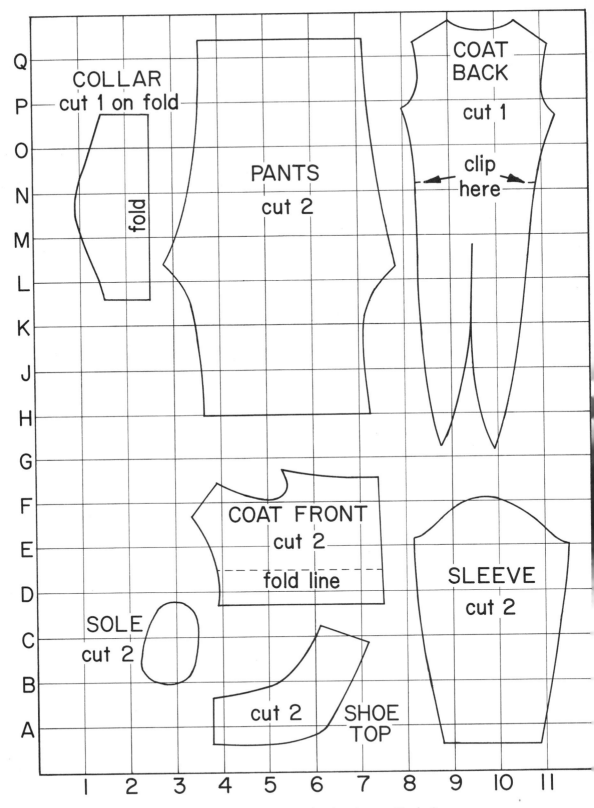

Fig. 11-2 Clothing pattern for dressing up Uncle Sam.

Figure 8   Historical characters are great fun to make. George Washington has a papier mâché head and Martha was made from an eggshell, while Uncle Sam has a head carved out of (what else?) soap!

Figure 9   Bread dough can be sculpted or molded to produce very professional looking dolls, like this skier.

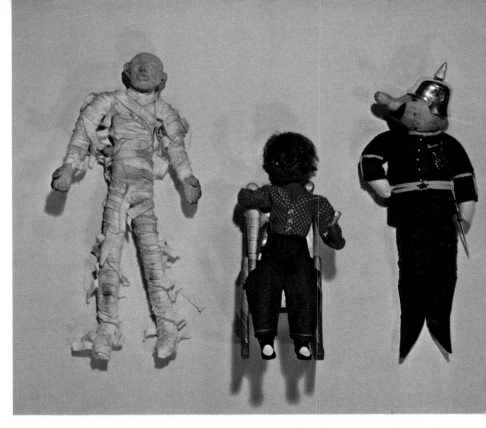

Figure 10 Papier mâché was used to mold the head for the mummy, the Rocking Chair Lush is a dried applehead and Kaiser Wilhelm is, basically, a long-nosed gourd.

Figure 11 With patience, truly life-like and delicate figures such as this farmer boy and his horse can be made by wrapping corn husks on wire armature bodies.

otherwise be visible between the lapels. Finally, stitch the beads on the front of the coat.

Shoes. Sew the back seam of each shoe top, then sew the shoe tops to the soles. Some cardboard stiffening can be placed over the sole inside the shoe so Uncle Sam won't lose his balance.

Accessories. The hair and beard are pieces of fluffed up cotton glued to the head and chin. The hat is a plastic one that can be bought at most craft and variety stores in several sizes. It, too, is glued to the head.

Chapter 12

Descendants of the Eminent Eggshell

Eggshell dolls, although not as fragile as you might think, are still not the sturdiest dolls in existence. They are usually for decoration and, just to play it safe, it's a good idea to arrange them in an out-of-the-way place where they cannot be brushed off the shelf too easily. On the other hand, if you don't mind a few casualties, you can make very nice centerpieces for any holiday gathering or party by standing a few simple eggheads around some central object. If the dolls aren't dropped or knocked about, they will last for many years. And even if they do get damaged, replacing the head is a fairly cheap and simple matter. For an idea of what an eggshell looks like with a little fancy dressing, see Figure 8 in the color section. Instructions and a pattern for that one—modeled after Martha Washington—are given later in this chapter.

Preparing Eggshells

BLOWING OUT THE EGG

The first step in making an eggshell doll is to get a reasonably whole and empty eggshell. For those few unfortunates who have never had the privilege of blowing out an egg for Easter, here's how it works.

First, use a darning needle or similar tool to carefully drill a hole in each end of the egg. Rotate the needle slowly, like a drill, to puncture the shell. Keep the hole small, no bigger than the pointed end of the darning needle, in the end of the egg you are going to use for the top of the head. Make the hole in the other end, the neck end, somewhat larger. Be sure to push the needle in far enough, when making the larger hole, to puncture the yolk sac. If you miss the yolk sac, all the blowing in the world won't get anything but the white out.

After you have both holes drilled, hold the egg over a bowl and blow gently into the small hole. It will take just a minute or two to empty the egg. The bowl full of egg innards, of course, is perfectly good and can be used for cooking.

DYEING

The simplest way of dyeing an eggshell is to use vegetable coloring or Easter egg dye. Because the eggshell is basically lime, however, you will have to add a tablespoon of vinegar to the dye so that the shell will be able to absorb the dye. Once the color is mixed and the vinegar added, just dip the blown-out shells into the dye and allow them to soak until they are about one shade darker than you want. "Overshoot" is necessary because the shell will continue to absorb the dye for some time after it is taken out of the dye bath. The final color, after drying, is therefore a bit lighter than the color when it was taken out of the dye.

A folksier, less commercial way of dyeing eggshells is with boiled onion skins. Simply put a handful of onion skins into a small saucepan, add enough water to cover your eggshells (which are not in the pan yet) and boil the onion skins for about five minutes. Now, put the eggshells in and simmer the whole thing until the shells are the shade of tan or brown that you prefer. For this, you don't need to add vinegar unless the shells start to develop a mottled, uneven appearance. In that case, add a teaspoon or so of vinegar and continue to simmer.

Whenever you use onion skin dye, particularly with the added vinegar, be sure you let your family know what you're doing. The dye smells a lot like very strong onion soup, but the taste is something else again. If anyone wandered into the kitchen while you were gone and tried tasting it, any reputation you might have had as a cook would go down the drain then and there. In fact, the dye might go down the drain, too, if the taster is on the impulsive side.

Another simple homemade dye—not quite as horrendous tasting as the onion skins—is strong tea or coffee. Simmer the eggshells in either of these until you get the shade you want. How dark they will get depends on how strong the coffee or tea is. As with the onion skin dye, a little vinegar will speed up the process and even out the coloring.

Whatever method you use, remember that the eggshells are fairly fragile: either simmer them very gently or turn off the heat altogether and let the shell stand in the hot dye. You can lift the shells out of the dye with a slotted spoon, but unless the eggs are getting too dark, I like to let the shells stay in the dye until everything has cooled off. This way, you can carefully remove the shells with your fingers. A spoon might scratch off some of the dye.

Once you have the shells out of the dye, let them dry in the air for 5 or 10 minutes.

PAINTING AND MOUNTING

For something as light and fragile as an eggshell, it's best to paint the features and hair on. Felt ink markers work quite well for both. If you wish, however, you can glue on a yarn or string wig. For the Martha Washington doll, I used some cotton. Whatever you use, remember to keep it light. If you would like to have the face a little shiny, coat the shell with clear nail polish or shellac after painting features on. A few eggshell faces are shown in Figure 12–1.

Because of the fragility of the eggshell, it is best to have the body completely dressed before mounting the head. Then just put a drop of glue on the neck wire of the body and place it up into the larger hole in the egg. If the hole is too large, try putting a little glue around the edges of the hole and, in effect, gluing the head to the shoulders.

Martha Washington

Materials

To make the eggshell doll shown in color (Fig. 8) and in Figure 12–2, you will need an eggshell head with appropriate features and hair, a wrapped wire body approximately 11 inches long and the following materials.

9″ x 27″ of velvet for skirt (no pattern supplied)
6″ x 7″ of brocade for dress top
11″ x 12″ of contrasting brocade for the drapes (the puffy pieces of
    material that overlay the gown)

Fig. 12–1 A sampling of painted eggshell faces, from a delicate-featured lady to an evil-looking villain.

11″ x 7″ of lace or organdy for scarf and sleeve ruffles
9″ x 34″ of white cotton for petticoat and pantalettes (cut pantalettes from pattern; cut a 9″ x 24″ square for petticoat)
6″ x 3″ of flesh-colored felt for arms and shoulders of body
cotton, for hair
40″ of black lace for trimming sleeves and scarf

ASSEMBLY

Enlarge the pattern in Figure 12–3 onto 1-inch square graph paper and cut out all fabric parts.

Finishing the Body. Because the bodice is cut a bit low, cover the top of the wrapped body with some flesh-colored felt. Extend the felt upward, like a tight turtleneck sweater collar, to fit around the bottom of the eggshell. Sew it into place, making your stitches as invisible as you can.

Sew the felt hands together and stuff them as tightly as you can. Do not stuff the arms above the wrists. Run a few stitches up between the "fingers" to give the hand a slightly more realistic appearance. Slide the felt arms up over the arms of the wrapped wire body and anchor them with a few stitches around the top.

Pantalettes. Hem the bottom of the legs of both halves, then sew the pieces together along one side, the inseam and the bottom half of the other side. Place the pantalettes on the doll and sew the rest of the side seam so that the top of the pantalettes fit snugly around her waist.

Fig. 12–2 Martha Washington in elegant Colonial gown.

Petticoat. Hem the bottom edge of the petticoat and sew up the back seam. Run a gathering thread around the top edge and place the petticoat on the body. Fasten the petticoat in place by pulling in the gathering thread and tying it.

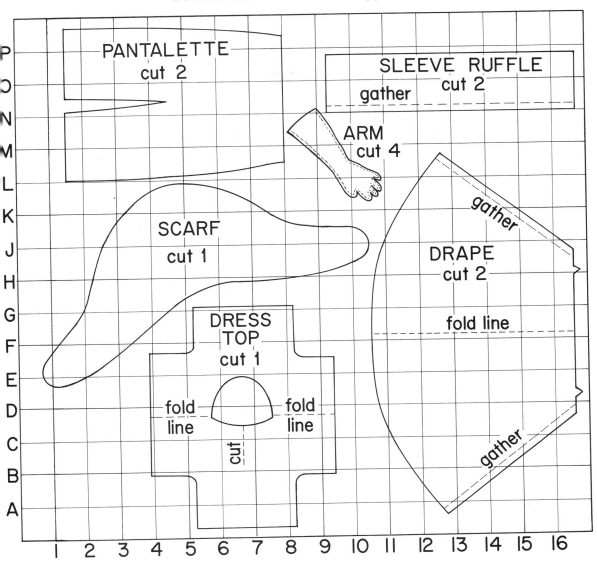

Fig. 12-3 Clothing pattern for Martha Washington: in addition to pattern parts supplied, cut two 9″ x 27″ rectangles—one of velvet for skirt, one of white cotton for petticoat.

Gown. Hem the bottom edge of the skirt and sew up the back seam. Run a gathering thread around the top edge of the skirt.

Hem the sleeve ruffles along the bottom edge and sew lace to the hemmed edges. Run a gathering thread around the top edge of the ruffles as indicated and sew them to the end of the sleeves, pulling in the gathers to fit. Once both ruffles are attached, fold the dress top along the shoulder line and sew the side and sleeve seams, including the ruffle seams. Finally, hem the neck. Do not place the gown on the doll yet.

Drapery. Hem the long, curved edge of each drapery piece. Fold each drapery in half along the fold line as shown, with the right sides on the inside. Stitch across the notched edge. Next turn the drapes right side out and run a gathering thread along what is now the top edge as indicated in Figure 12–3. Pull the gathers in so that the top edge of each drape stretches approximately half way around the body, from midfront to midback, and sew to the bottom of the dress top.

Sew the bodice, with the drapes attached, to the top of the skirt. Place the gown on the doll and sew up the back opening in the bodice.

Accessories. Hem entirely around the edge of the scarf and sew on the lace trim. Place the scarf around the doll's shoulders, the two ends overlapping each other in the front. Pin the scarf in place.

The hair is made of pieces of fluffed up cotton glued to the head. Some tiny plastic flowers tied into a bouquet with a narrow ribbon are fastened to her hair.

Chapter 13

Bread Dough Characters

It may sound odd at first, but bread dough can give you a chance to be really creative. You can mold it as you do clay, only more easily. It's softer and easier to shape than clay, but when properly coated and baked, it has the hardness and sheen of ceramic. It will also break just as quickly as ceramic, so it can't be used for play dolls. Bread dough can, however, be made into beautiful collectors' dolls and some dolls of this type command very high prices and are in great demand. The skier shown in Figure 9 in the color section is a typical (for me) example. It will never be a collectors' item, but it was fun to make. Patterns and instructions for the skier are given later in this chapter.

Working with Bread Dough

MAKING DOUGH

To make enough modeling dough for one doll like the skier and preserve the results, you will need the following.

4 slices of fresh white bread
4 tablespoons of white glue, such as Elmer's
acrylic paint or vegetable coloring
glycerine (obtained at any drugstore)

PROCEDURE

Discard the crusts from the bread and shred the slices into the smallest pieces you can. Add the glue and mix with your hands until the mixture no longer sticks to your hands. (This is awfully messy for awhile, but just keep on kneading; it will eventually turn out the way it is supposed to.)

Next, add the coloring. If you're using regular acrylic paint, dip a stick into the paint and then poke the stick into the dough. The paint will stay in the dough when you remove the stick. If you use vegetable coloring, just put a few drops onto the dough. Whichever type of coloring you use, simply knead the dough until the color is evenly distributed, adding small amounts to get the shade you want.

MODELING

As soon as you have the dough the color you want it, add about 10 drops of glycerine and work it into the dough as you did the paint: you're ready to start modeling. If you don't use the dough fairly soon—within a few hours— you will have to store it in something to keep it from drying and becoming unworkable. If you're going to keep it for a long time, it can be frozen.

I'm not sure how professionals do the modeling, but with me it is mostly trial and error. I just take a chunk of dough and pinch and poke until it starts to look like a head. Once it has roughly the shape I'm after, I smooth down the surface by putting a little glycerine on my fingers and rubbing it over the head. Beads pressed directly into the face make fairly good eyes. For the rest of the features, though, you're on your own. If you want to use a stuffed body, you will have to insert a neck flange at this point. When you have the dough in the shape you want, let it dry for 2 or 3 days.

If you don't feel like modeling an original face, you can always make a molded head instead. To do this, cut a discarded plastic doll head apart, from ear to ear over the top of the head. Coat the inside with salad oil or glycerine, then push some of the dough into the inside of both halves. When the dough feels fairly dry (usually after a couple of days), carefully remove it from the molds and let it dry in the open for another day or two. Then attach the head pieces with white glue and allow to dry.

Although it isn't necessary, I like to make the hands and feet of the doll from dough, too. It makes the finished doll look more professional, if that's what you're aiming for—and mine need all the help they can get.

COATING

Once the sculpted or molded dough parts have dried, coat them with a mixture of equal parts of white glue and water. You can rub the mixture on with your fingers or use a soft, rather large artist's brush. You will need at least three coats of this mixture, which turns into a glaze as it dries. Allow the articles to stand out in the air for several hours to dry between coats. How long it takes to dry depends on the weather, so if you're impatient, you can touch it every so often in an inconspicuous spot to see if it's dry.

BAKING AND ASSEMBLING

Place the coated dough forms on a cookie sheet or an aluminum tray and bake at 350 degrees for 3 to 4 minutes. Very little baking is actually done in that short time, of course, but the heat seems to sterilize the dough and retards the growth of mold. The surface that is in contact with the cookie sheet, though, may start to brown a bit. If your molded head is larger than the one for the skier (about $1\frac{1}{2}$ inches in diameter), lower the temperature and increase the baking time correspondingly. A 3-inch head, for instance, would probably require 10 minutes at about 250 degrees.

Take the dough from the oven and let it partially cool. When it's cooled enough so you can handle it easily, push the body wires into the dough. If you don't have a complete wire armature body, you can stick plain wires into the dough parts as shown in Figure 13–1. These wires can be easily attached to a wire body later. The wires have to be added fairly soon after baking, because the surface becomes hard in a half hour or so.

Once the drying is complete, you can add features with any kind of paint. After the features are on, you can further seal the surface with another coat of glue-and-water glaze or a coat of clear shellac. Let it dry for a few hours and the dough parts of the doll are complete.

If you wish to make a doll with a stuffed body instead of a wire body, a flange was inserted in the freshly modeled dough. The flange can be placed inside the neck of a stuffed body and held in place by tightening the cloth around the top of the flange with a string.

Bread Dough Skier

Materials

To make the bread dough skier, you will need the bread dough head (and arms and feet, if you wish), a wrapped wire body approximately 9 inches long and the following materials.

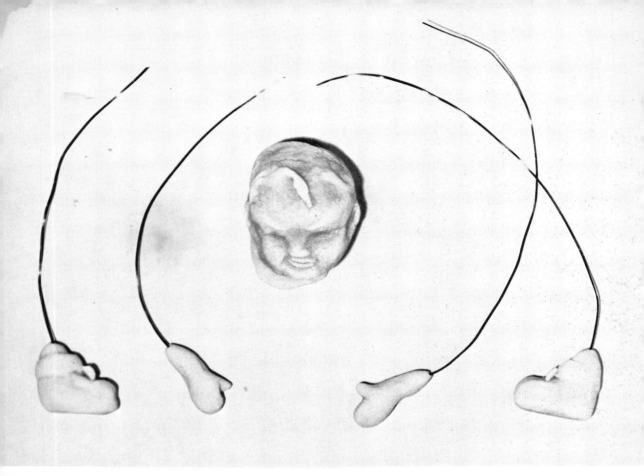

Fig. 13–1   Bread dough head, hands and feet are mounted on wire before the final drying stage.

7½"x13" of black felt for pants
12" x 16" of knit material for sweater, muffler, and gloves
a colorful pompom
2" x 25" strip of white fabric for "cast"
2 pieces of masonite, 1" diameter
2 craft sticks
2 round sticks, 6" length

ASSEMBLY

Enlarge the pattern in Figure 13–2 onto 1-inch square graph paper and cut out all fabric parts.

Pants. Since the pants are made of felt, no hemming is required. Place the front and back halves together and sew the side seams. Place the trousers on the doll and sew up the inseam. With the pants on the doll, either make darts in the top of the pants to make them fit snugly or pad out the body. When the pants fit the way you want, stitch them to the body.

Sweater. Hem the ends of the sleeves, then fold the sweater on the

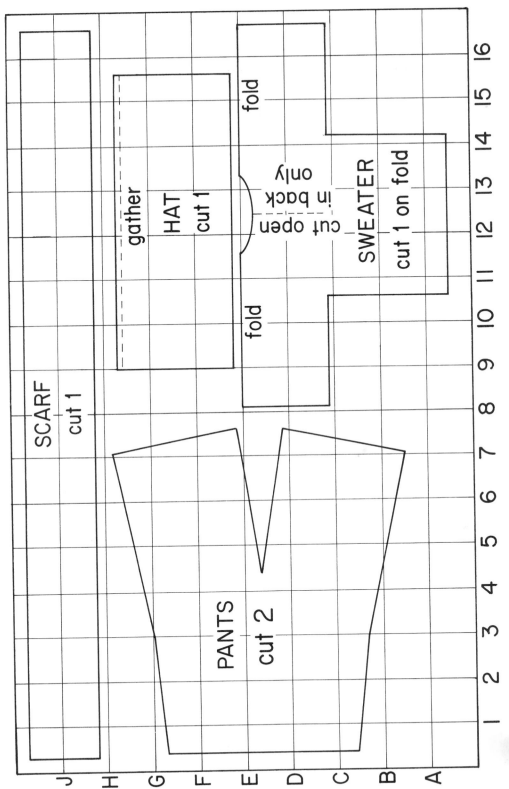

Fig. 13-2 Clothing pattern for the bread dough skier, replete with leg cast.

shoulder line and sew the sleeve and side seams. Hem the bottom of the sweater and place it on the doll, over the pants. Pad the body to fill out the sweater if necessary and sew up the back seam.

Hat and Muffler. Hem around the bottom of the hat piece, then sew up the back seam using an overcast or a buttonhole stitch. Gather the top of the hat together like a stocking cap and fasten the gathers in place. Sew a pompom (Ch. 4) in the center of the top, over the gathering point.

Hem the two long edges of the muffler. If possible, stitch across each end a half inch or so from the edge, then unravel some of the material beyond the stitching. The idea is to make the ends look like fringe. If this isn't practical, hem the two ends the same as the sides. To fasten it to the skier, simply knot it around his neck.

Accessories. The ski poles are round sticks with round pieces of masonite with their centers drilled out. The masonite pieces are shoved over the sticks and glued in place.

The skis are craft sticks, which you can get in any hobby store. To make them look like skis, I sharpened one end and soaked the sticks until the wood could be bent. Once they were bent, they retained the shape when they dried.

The shoes are something I swiped from a commercial doll some time in the past. You can make your own from the pattern in Figure 4–9, though, if you need to. The laces I used are lengths of rawhide boot laces, cut in half lengthwise.

The cast is simply a long strip of white fabric wrapped four or five times around the leg and stitched in place along the back of the leg.

To make it look like he is wearing gloves, stitch a couple of small pieces of knit material over the hands and pull the sleeves of the sweater down so that only the knit fabric (and not the wrapped wire arms) shows.

Chapter 14

Dried Fruit Druids

If the number of articles that have appeared recently in magazines and news-papers is any indication, the dried apple doll must be the most popular folk art doll in the country. One reason, I suppose, is that the finished product is always a surprise. No matter what sort of face you carve in the fresh apple, it bears little resemblance to what emerges after a few weeks of drying and shriveling. You can hang a relatively handsome, Roman-nosed character up to dry and come back a month later to find something that would make Quasimoto look like a matinee idol.

Personally, I like them because they are great equalizers of carving talent. As long as I stick to a couple of simple rules, my fumble-fingered whittling, when dried up suitably, looks just as good—or just as bad, depending on your taste in grotesquerie—as anything that a real craftsman or sculptor could turn out.

Also, and maybe more important, I just happen to like bizarre looking creatures and dried apple heads are nothing if not weird. If you don't believe me, take a look at the three examples in Figure 14-1, projects also shown in color (Figs. 10 and 14). There are instructions for making all three later in this chapter.

Working with Fruit

You don't have to limit yourself to apples, although they are certainly the most common. Pears are rapidly becoming my own favorite. Based on the few I've done recently, they have a special character all their own. Prunes are also a possibility, particularly if you're an old Dick Tracy fan. They don't require much drying, of course, but the amount of carving you need to do is also very slight.

Whether you use apples or pears, always look for firm, slightly less than ripe fruit. You don't want them actually green, though. About the only way of finding the right fruit is by trial and error. Get a batch that is still green and keep a close eye on them. Start carving one every day or so. Pretty soon you'll find one that is just right. Actually, as long as the peeled fruit isn't soft to the touch, it should work out reasonably well. It's just that certain consistencies are somewhat easier to work with than others.

Fig. 14-1   A sampling of dried fruit dolls. From left, Shrunken Head, Druidian Monk and a Rocking Chair Lush.

As for the type of fruit, I find that, among apples, the Golden Delicious shrinks up about the best of all the varieties. The best type of pear is the hard winter variety. Softer fruit, like a MacIntosh apple, has too much juice and will shrink away to practically nothing. Any of the drier, more mealy apples will probably work fairly well.

CARVING

The first thing to do after peeling the fruit is to rub lemon juice all over it. If you have enough juice, dip the whole fruit into it and let it soak for a few minutes. This will keep the fruit from browning too fast. Also, after you have finished the carving, you should repeat the treatment, so save the lemon juice. You can use powdered citric acid dissolved in water, instead of lemon juice. If you skip this treatment, the apple either rots or turns black rather rapidly instead of just shrinking and warping.

When carving, make large, exaggerated features—huge noses, protruding ears, deeply excavated eyes, etc. This way, there's a chance that when the drying is complete, the features won't have shrunk completely out of sight and one or two may even bear a faint similarity to what you carved. Three apples and a pear that I carved a few weeks ago are shown in Figures 14–2 and 14–3. What happened to three of them is shown in Figure 14–4. Oddly enough, a few of the features are still halfway recognizable on the apples. In fact, now that I think about it, the dried fruits are, in some cases, somewhat like caricatures of the original carvings. In case you're wondering how the other apple in the illustrations turned out, look again at Figure 14–1.

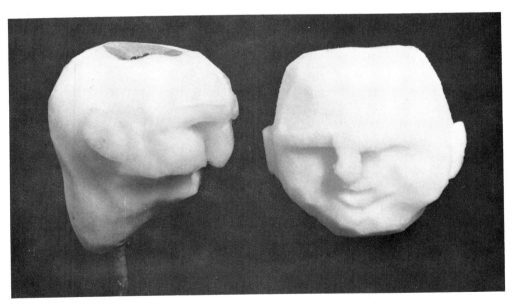

Fig. 14–2 Freshly carved pear (left) and apple heads.

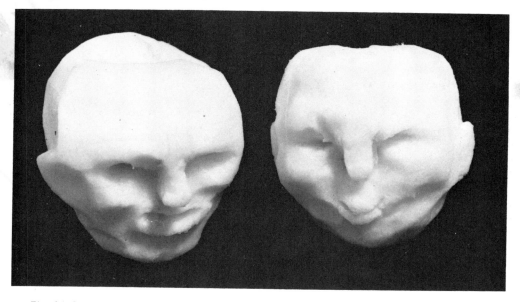

Fig. 14–3 Variations of the exaggerated features you carve when working with fruit.

One more tip on carving: if you intend to put an actual eyeball of some kind into the eye socket, put it in at the same time you do the carving. This way, the apple will dry up around the bead or whatever you use for the eye and hold it in place. (Any small dark thing, like a clove, a bead, even a soy bean, works quite well for an eye.) After the head has dried, you can put a dot of paint on each eyeball for a highlight.

Fig. 14–4 Apple and pear carvings after drying a few weeks—yeeks!

DRYING

When the head has been carved and lemon juiced to your satisfaction, push a stick into the neck end of the fruit, tie a string to the stick and hang the head upside down in a warm, dry place that is reasonably free from drafts. I use a corner of my pantry to hang up my heads, but anyplace that doesn't get damp or drafty will do. Too much dampness (as in a basement) will make the fruit turn moldy. If the weather turns particularly humid for a day or two, the head will probably begin to soften, but unless the humidity stays high for several days, the apple will harden up again when the air dries out. As for drafts, I have no idea why, but every time I tried hanging the apples in a drafty spot, they got moldy.

How long the drying takes depends on conditions, but 4 to 6 weeks is enough under almost any circumstances. It will go faster in cold weather, when the heat is on in the house and the air is dry. The only drawback to cold-weather drying is that the fruit, by then, is probably not fresh but taken from storage. For apples, this doesn't make a lot of difference, but pears tend to get too soft and will shrink too much when they dry.

PAINTING AND PRESERVING

When the head is dry, pull out the stick and add whatever paint you want. The color of the fruit will vary from very light to dark brown, depending on how much lemon juice you put on it. As with some of the other heads, you can use lipstick on a cotton swab to tint the cheeks if you wish. Again, be careful not to get tiny chunks of lipstick in the cotton, since this will give you a streaked look rather than a light, even tone. Small dots of white paint can add highlights to the eyes, too.

A dried fruit doll with no more preparation than what we've already discussed will last several years, though they will usually petrify in time without further treatment. If you want to preserve them a bit longer, or if you want to add a glossy sheen to the surface, coat the entire head with clear nail polish or shellac.

MOUNTING

Let the head dry a day or two after painting and coating it, before adding hair and putting the head on a body.

As with so many other heads, the wrapped wire body works very well with dried fruit heads. In this case, make the neck wire longer than usual, say at least an inch, so that it will stick well up into the apple and hold firmly. Once the head is on the body, fill up the neck hole and the hole from the core on top of the head with plastic wood, papier mâché or something similar.

After the filling has dried, you can add hair and clothes. Somehow, yarn and thread wigs don't seem to go well with most appleheads, although there is one exception I'll mention in the following project. My own favorite hair is fur or cotton, both of which are quite easy to glue on.

Shrunken Head

If you don't feel like making a body and if you have a slightly odd turn of mind, you could make the item shown in Figure 14–5. It strikes me that a shrunken head is something quite appropriate to make from a dried apple.

Start the shrunken head by carving the apple just as you would for a normal doll, except leave the eyes pretty well closed or make slits. Then, instead of putting beads into the eye depressions, cut small vertical slits just above the eyes and stick pieces of false eyelash or very fine black thread in the slits so they extend down over the eyes. As with normal dolls, be sure to treat the head with lemon juice before and after carving.

Now let the head partially dry. Wait until it has shrunken somewhat, but not until it is so hard you can't still indent it with your fingers: then push rice kernels into the mouth for teeth. At the same time, if you want to be really authentic, use a very small sharp needle to run some black thread through the lips and let it dangle, as shown in Figure 14–5. When the head is completely dry, fill in the holes on the top and bottom of the head, just as you do with the other dolls.

Raven black, shiny hair looks best on shrunken heads. What I used on this one was a small piece from an old, full-sized wig. Just take a clump of hair (or black thread if you don't have hair) about 6 inches long and tie it together at one end. Glue the tied end to the top of the head. When the glue has set, push a black thumbtack through the hair and thread into the head. Spread the hair around so that it hangs down in all directions except directly over the face, then spot a little glue around the edges to keep the hair lying in generally the right directions.

To suspend the head, attach a string or wire to the thumbtack and hang it—well, hang it wherever you would like to have a shrunken head hanging . . .

Druidian Monk

To make the monk shown in color (Fig. 14) and in Figure 14–1, all you need to do is make a suitably terrified-looking dried pear head, glue a little bristly fur on top for hair, fasten it to a small wrapped wire body and wrap the body bulkily in lots of dark brown chiffon. On this particular one, the chiffon is held in place by a large rubber band around the waist. I'm not sure what the candle is. It was another item from my odds and ends box, the origin of which I've long since forgotten.

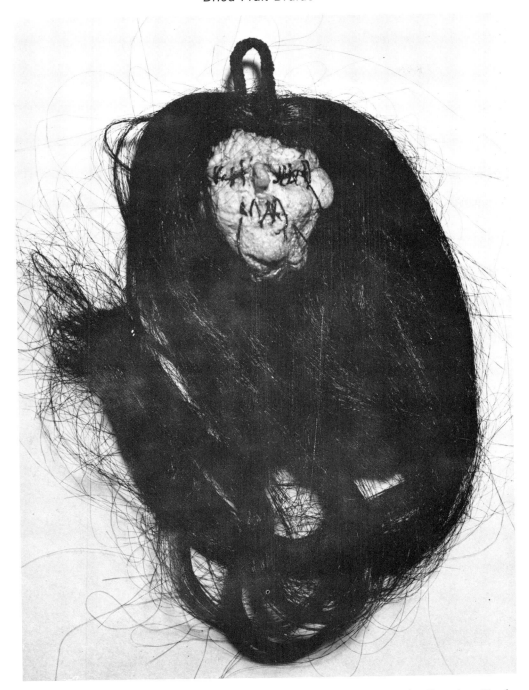

Fig. 14–5 Remnants of an old wig are used to make an eerie wig for the Shrunken Head.

Rocking Chair Lush

Materials

To make this doll, shown in color Figure 10 and in Figure 14–1, you need a dried apple head, some fur for the wig, a wrapped wire body about nine inches long and the following materials.

9″ square of print or gingham fabric for shirt and cuffs
9″ x 10″ of contrasting fabric, for pants
approximately 2″ x 4″ of dark fabric for scarf

ASSEMBLY

Cut all parts according to the pattern in Figure 14–6 after enlarging the pattern onto 1-inch square graph paper.

Scarf. Wrap the 2″ x 4″ piece of fabric around the neck and upper body and anchor it with a couple of stitches in the back. The scarf covers the part of the wrapped body that would show through the open collar of the shirt.

Shirt. Fold each shirt front piece on the fold line as shown (Fig. 14–6) and run a line of stitching close to the fold on each side. Next, sew the two pieces of shirt front to the shirt back along the shoulder seams all the way down the sleeve. With the shirt partially assembled this way, run a gathering thread along the edge of the sleeve ends, then pull up the gathers so that the width of the sleeve end is equal to the width of the cuff. Sew the cuffs to the gathered sleeve ends and hem the cuffs. Turn the neckline under and stitch it.

Sew up the underneath sleeve seams and the side seams. Place the shirt on the doll and stitch up the front opening to within about an inch of the top. Fold that part back like lapels and sew some kind of buttons to the shirt front.

Pants. Place the right and left halves of the pants together and sew the front and back center seams, then hem the bottoms of the legs. Turn under the waist and stitch. Then sew the inseams. Place the pants on the doll over the shirt and either take in darts to make the pants fit the body or pad out the body. Stitch the top of the pants to the body and the bottom of the shirt.

Accessories. The shoes and glasses are both items I swiped from commercial dolls. The glass in his hand is a piece of rolled-up foil stitched to the hand. The glasses can be hand-fashioned from light, thin wire with a little patience. You can make your own shoes using the pattern and instructions in Chapter 4 (see Fig. 4–9). The buttons on the shirt are beads.

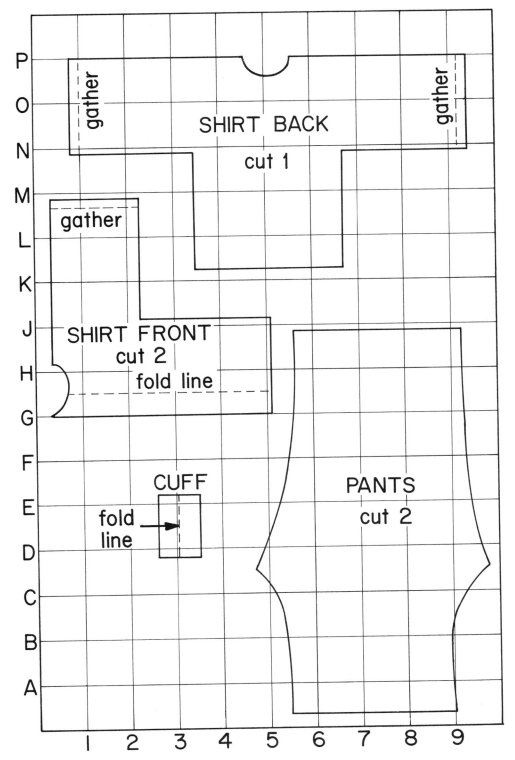

Fig. 14–6 Clothing pattern for the Rocking Chair Lush.

Chapter 15

Rawhide
Babies

Rawhide babies are dolls made of leather, such as the one in Figure 15–1. They aren't necessarily babies: that's just what they're called, for whatever the reason. They were originally made by Eskimos and American Indians, but not many authentic ones still exist outside of museum collections. In fact, very few leather dolls of any kind have survived great lengths of time. I suspect it's because leather has a couple of natural enemies, dampness and rats, either of which can do in an unprotected doll rather rapidly.

Working with Leather

If you want to be really authentic, you would have to stuff this doll with dried grass or moss. If you aren't that much of a stickler or if you have hay fever, almost any stuffing will do. You could even, for instance, use the lint from your clothes dryer, if you happen to have saved that sort of thing. (I didn't until I started stuffing a lot of dolls; lately I've been saving it all.)

Fig. 15–1 Rawhide Eskimo is dressed in fur for the long cold winters.

SELECTING

Finding leather for the doll may be a problem. Remember, it has to be quite soft and thin and pliable. So far I've made all of mine out of deerskin, since I lucked out a couple of years ago and found some whole deerskins on sale at a local flea market for only five dollars apiece. I got two, and that's enough deerskin for a half dozen dolls the size of the one you'll be making in this chapter. Other possible sources are old deerskin vests or jackets, which you can occasionally find in rummage sales. (Don't worry if the jacket looks soiled; the inside is most likely clean enough to use.) Or if you don't mind the higher prices, you could get what you want at most leather shops and craft shops. You could even go to a hardware or department store and pick up some chamois, which also works quite well.

SEWING

For the type of leather used for these dolls, you will be using a regular "inside out" seam, so it is easier by far if you can use a sewing machine. It's not essential, but it will save a lot of wear and tear on your fingers. While the leather is soft enough to allow you to force the needle through, it is still tough enough to make it quite a chore. On the other hand, punching holes first isn't too practical for seams like this. For one thing, with large holes you would have trouble getting the seam as tight as you would like. For another, that's a lot of holes to punch.

Deerhide has a rough and a smooth side. When sewing, place the smooth sides together so that, when the item is turned inside out, the smooth side will be outside. The soft leather surface gives a pleasant, lifelike smoothness to the doll's skin.

If you are using the leather for clothes and you want to make fringes along the seams, like the buckskin that Indians and pioneers wore, simply leave a large seam allowance and don't turn the seam inside out. Then cut the seam allowance into fringe.

With leather, large stitches work better than small ones for a couple of reasons. For one, you need fewer of them, which means less wear and tear on your fingers if you're doing it by hand. A more practical reason is that, if you get the stitches too close together, you will weaken the leather. You need only enough stitches to hold the stuffing in. Just be sure the thread you use is strong.

FACES AND DECORATIONS

Keep this doll as simple as possible. For a face, a few beads sewn on for eyes and mouth are more compatible with the rest of the doll than an elaborate, professional looking paint job. (An unspectacular example is shown in

Fig. 15–2.) The type of face depends on what you're going to use the doll for. If it's for a child who might want to take it in for "show and tell," the face should be relatively smooth and modern looking. If you plan to peddle it to a doll collector, on the other hand, something a little cruder might be better. If you're like me, you don't have that much choice: mine usually end up looking somewhat crude, no matter what my original intentions were.

If you want to go to a bit more trouble, you could always mold the leather into a face, using the same basic procedure described for making molded felt faces in Chapter 17. (In fact, if you wanted to fudge a bit or if you have trouble finding the right kind of leather, you could make an imitation rawhide baby out of felt.)

Leather Eskimo

Materials

To make an approximation of the Eskimo doll in Figure 15–1, you will need the following materials.

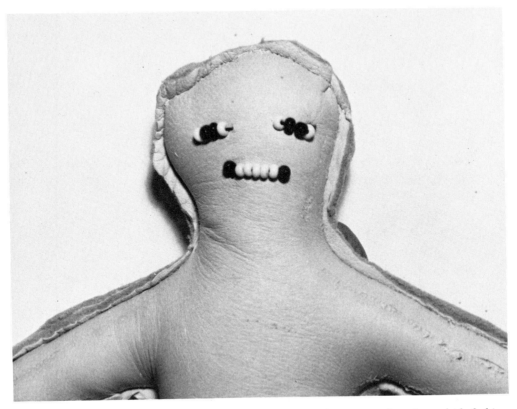

Fig. 15–2 Sewing beads onto the face for features makes the most authentic rawhide babies.

36" x 18" of soft leather for doll body

15" x 30" of dark long-haired fur, for parka and for trim around front
   of hood

9" x 14" of contrasting color, short-haired fur for main part of hood
   and for gloves

1 lb. stuffing material

10" strip of fur, about 1½" wide, for simulated boot tops

15" strip of decorative braid for parka trimming

Enlarge both patterns given (Figs. 15–3 and 15–4) and cut all parts according to the body and clothes patterns. Refer back to Chapter 4 for special instructions on cutting fur.

BODY ASSEMBLY

Head. The head has three pieces, one for the face and two for the back of the head. Having two pieces for the back gives the head more of a "head shape." However, if you prefer a more primitive look, just cut out two head pieces and use a single piece for the back. If the head is molded, use an overcast stitch. Otherwise, use the standard inside out seam.

Legs. Each leg is also made up of three pieces. The two halves of the lower leg are sewn together and then the upper leg strip is sewn around the top of the lower leg, all using the standard seam. Leave the *top* of each leg open for stuffing. I used three pieces for the legs primarily to keep from wasting leather. You can cut these smaller pieces from scraps of leather that, otherwise, you might not be able to use. On the other hand, if you have all the leather you want, you can extend the lower leg pattern upward and make the legs from two larger pieces instead of three smaller ones.

Torso and Arms. The torso and arms each consist of two identical pieces, sewn together with the standard seam. Leave the following spots open for stuffing: the neck section of the torso; the neck of the head; the shoulder end of the arms.

Body Assembly. Stuff all the parts, but sew shut only the arms and legs. Leave the neck openings of the head and torso open and sew the head to the torso using an overcast stitch. As you stitch, continue to poke stuffing into the neck so that when you finish the neck will be stuffed firmly and the head will not be too wobbly. Sew the stuffed limbs onto the body after they have been stitched shut. Unlike the head, the limbs will be quite floppy where they are attached to the body.

Before you put any clothes on the doll, add whatever type of face and hair that you want. Just remember if you use oil paint to let it dry for several days before doing anything else to the doll. If it's the least bit damp, it will very likely get smudged when you work with the hood, which fits snugly around the head.

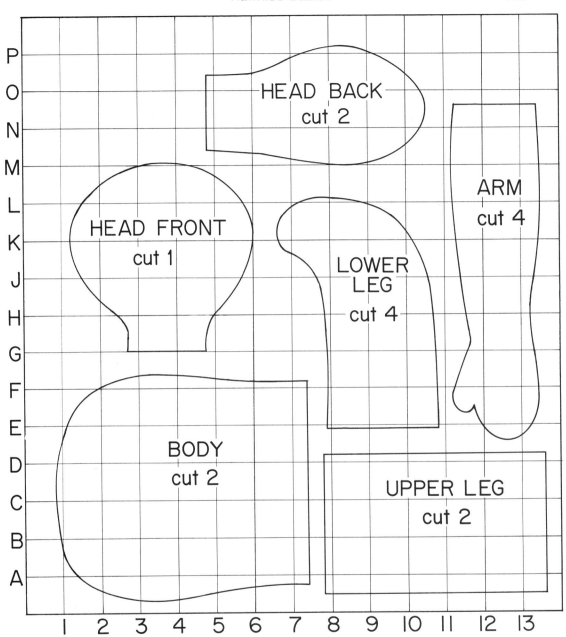

Fig. 15–3 Body parts pattern for Rawhide Eskimo.

CLOTHING

Parka. With fur, of course, no hemming is required, so the first step is to fold the parka along the shoulder line and sew up the sleeve and side seams using a ladder stitch (see Fig. 2–3D). Next, sew the back and top (the curved edges) of the hood together. Sew the bottom of the hood to the edge of the

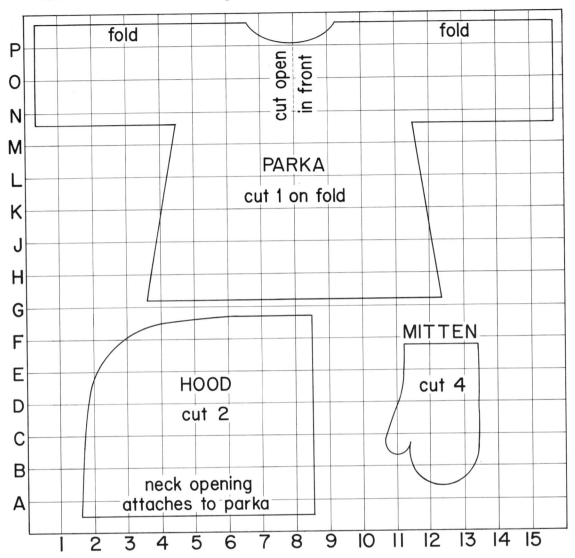

Fig. 15–4 Clothing pattern for the Eskimo rawhide baby.

neck opening in the parka, then sew a strip of fur matching the parka completely along the front edge of the hood. If you want the decoration, sew a strip
of decorative braid around the parka about a half inch up from the bottom
edge. (You could use a strip from a beaded or braided belt.) Place the parka and
hood on the doll and sew up the back neck opening of the parka.

Accessories. Sew the mitten pieces together and place mittens on the
hands. They should fit tightly enough to stay on without any stitching.

Finally, wrap the two 1½-inch strips of fur around the legs about where
the knees might be (or over the junction between the upper and lower leg
sections). Sew the ends of each strip together tightly enough to keep the strips
in place.

Chapter 16

Papier Mâché People

Papier mâché has several advantages: it's easy to work with, dries hard and light, takes paint well and is quite durable. Also, even if your sculpting ability is practically nonexistent, you can still make a somewhat professional looking doll by using an old doll head for a mold. Mâché is also quite inexpensive. Commercial mixes, like Celluclay®, are available at most craft and variety stores for a dollar or so for a pound package, which is enough for a dozen dolls or more. On the other hand, if you really want to start from scratch, you can make your own mâché from a tube or bottle of white glue, some water and a couple of old newspapers. That's not only less expensive, but it gives you a feeling of having really done the whole thing yourself. A couple of my creations are shown in Figure 16-1. The dignified looking guy, who's supposed to be George Washington, and the mummy, are also shown in Figures 8 and 10 in the color section.

Fig. 16–1   A selection of dolls with heads molded in papier mâché: from left, George Washington, a babydoll and a ghastly mummy.

Working with Papier Mâché

MAKING THE MIX

Making your own mâché is not particularly difficult, but it is particularly messy, even more so than bread dough. You can use almost any relatively flimsy paper: newspapers, bathroom tissue, the less durable, unreinforced paper towels, etc. Slick paper, the kind you find in many magazines, has been treated so it won't absorb water and doesn't work at all.

Start by tearing the paper into tiny bits, the smaller the better. About 4 of the double-size newspaper sheets (16 pages) is about enough for your average doll head, but if you plan to make another doll sometime, it's best to make larger batches. Mâché will keep indefinitely. Put the shredded paper into a pail of water and let it stand for at least an hour, preferably overnight.

Once the paper has become sufficiently globby and waterlogged, pick up a mass of it in your hands. Let some of the water drain off, squeeze the pulp a

Figure 12   The more elaborate and historically accurate the garments, the more they contrast with the ludicrous gourd heads: witness Henry VIII and Elizabeth I.

Figure 13   The pilgrim and peasant girl are traditional all-husk dolls with corn silk hair and husk clothing.

Figure 14   Carved, dried fruits are perfect for shrunken heads, strange Druids and other evil-looking characters.

Figure 15   A delightful array of beady eyed and easy-to-make yarn critters.

little (but don't pack it into too tight a ball) and put the resulting blob into an electric blender (you can use a manual rotary egg beater, but it's harder). Turn the blender on medium speed for a minute or so, until the paper is thoroughly pulverized and mixed. Pour the pulverized paper into a colander and put the next handful into the blender; keep going until you've used up all the paper.

With the pulverized paper in the colander, squeeze to remove a bit more of the water, then let it set for a day or so. It should still be a little soupy at this point.

For each quart of mixture, add about 4 tablespoons of white glue and a tablespoon of some kind of oil, such as linseed oil, mineral oil or glycerine. The oil seems to retard the growth of mold, and make the mixture feel smoother. If you don't have enough glue, you can substitute flour and water or wallpaper paste (wheat paste). You would need one and a half times as much flour as you would of glue. Now mix the resulting mess very well. Use your hands to knead it like bread dough until you're sure everything is thoroughly blended and feels smooth to the touch. The color—unless you've used colored tissue paper to make your mix—will probably be a dull, uniform grey.

Now you can add a preservative if you wish. If you're going to make solid, sculpted heads from your mâché, you will certainly need a preservative. (Solid heads take so long to dry that without the preservative they would probably mildew.) Molded heads, on the other hand, don't usually give you that problem. I usually use formaldehyde, which you can get at any drugstore. The only problem is the odor, which—though it will go away as the mâché dries —is a bit much at first. For sweeter smelling mâché, you could use oil of wintergreen or oil of cloves, also available at drugstores. I use about a teaspoonful of preservative to a quart of mâché mixture. Once it's added, knead the mixture until it's blended in.

STORING

Mâché without a preservative added will start to mildew after about two days at room temperature, even if it is stored in a jar or plastic bag. In a refrigerator, it will keep for a couple of weeks. Kept in the open, either kind will start to dry after a few hours or a day. If you want to keep either kind a long time, simply put it in a container and freeze it. Freezing doesn't seem to affect the mâché in any way. When you're ready to use it, just let it thaw, knead it a little and it will be just like fresh.

MOLDING HEADS AND BODIES

Molded heads and bodies can be made to look quite professional, if that's what you're after. There are two things to remember in selecting a doll to use as a mold. First, the doll itself will be disassembled and the individual parts cut in two, so you had better pick a doll you don't have any further use for. Second, mâché shrinks during drying to about two thirds of its original size. Thus, if you want a doll with a head 2 inches wide, the doll you use for a mold will need a head about 3 inches wide.

Once you've selected the doll, pull off its head and any other parts you plan to use as molds. On each separate part, there is a small ridge running completely around it. This is the mold line, which was formed when the doll parts themselves were molded. Using an X-acto knife or a single-edged razor blade, cut the parts in two along the mold lines. Next, inspect the inside of the doll parts. To make a good mold, the inside has to be smooth, with the features plainly indented into the surface. Sometimes the eye and nose holes are filled with plastic, in which case the doll would be useless as a mold.

One other possibility would be to make a plaster mold of the outside of the doll face and use that for a mold. To do this, mix a small batch of plaster of paris in a small container, such as a margarine tub, then oil the doll's face and press it down into the wet plaster. Leave the doll head in the plaster for a day or so, until the plaster has set firmly. Repeat the same procedure for the back of the head.

Before putting the mâché mixture into a mold, grease the mold thoroughly with mineral oil. (Vegetable oils would turn rancid in a day or so.) Be sure to grease all the nooks and crannies, not just the large, open areas in the mold. Similarly, when putting the mâché into the mold, push the mix solidly into all the ends and small spots, especially the nose and—if you mold the hands as well—the fingers.

Drying in the open air will take a week or more, normally. If you have an oven with a pilot light, you can do as I do and leave the mâché-filled mold in the oven with only the pilot light on for 2 or 3 days. Just be sure you put a sign on the oven controls so no one (including yourself) will inadvertently bake your molds. If you don't have a gas oven and you're in a hurry, you could try turning the oven to about 200 degrees, putting the molds in for 2 or 3 hours, then turning the oven off and leaving the molds inside until the oven has reached room temperature. Whatever method you use, be careful about taking the mâché out of the forms before it has completely dried. If it is a uniform, light color, it is probably dry. If there are any darker spots, it isn't. Even if it does look dry, it's a good idea to give it a little more time before taking it out of the mold. If it isn't completely dry, there is a good chance that, even with all the grease you put in the mold, some of the mâché will stick to the inside of the mold. In fact, it happens to me so often that this is one reason I usually try to sculpt my heads, no matter what they look like. They may not look as good as a molded one, but there's no chance they will fall apart, and they're more fun, anyway. The molding can get to be a chore after a couple of potential heads have left little pieces of themselves inside the doll head.

SCULPTING PAPIER MÂCHÉ

Papier mâché is modeled the same way clay and bread dough are. Just remember that the head will shrink to about two thirds of its original size when it dries. Make a ball of the mâché, squeeze it to get out any air bubbles, put a stick into one end and mount the whole affair in an old egg carton or anything that will give you a base to keep the stick upright. If you're a sculptor, then, you start sculpting. If you're like me, you just poke and pull at the mâché until it starts looking like a face you could learn to love. Once you have it the way you want it, just let it dry for at least a week. Again, you could use a pilot lighted oven, but this will take longer than for the molded mâché because the sculpted head is solid, not just a thick coating over the inside of the mold.

If you want to keep the weight and drying time down, you could use a Styrofoam ball or a thread spool as a core instead of making a head of solid mâché. This seems to work well enough and it also cuts down on shrinkage. In fact, whole bodies can be made this way, using lighter objects as cores and covering them with thick layers of mâché.

FINISHING AND PAINTING

When the mâché has dried, it will be rather rough, perhaps even wrinkled, as is the one in Figure 16–2. I left this one as is because he seemed to fit the body I made for him, but I usually sand them down with a very fine sandpaper. This is a slow process, though, because you have to be very careful not to break off any features. If, in the end, you can't get all the wrinkles out, you could always add a smidgin of 50–50 mixture of plaster of paris and white glue, with a little water if necessary. To apply this, use a small brush and paint it all over the head. Allow it to dry. This will make about as smooth a finish as you can get and it will also serve as protection for the head.

When the surface has been prepared to your satisfaction, paint the features on. The hair can be painted on or you can glue a wig on. If you want a glossy finish, you can always shellac the face after the features have dried. The shellac would also protect it against water, if you think the doll will need it. Uncoated mâché, though, is quite resistant to ordinary hazards like heat, cold and direct sunlight.

MOUNTING

I usually prefer wrapped wire bodies, particularly for sculpted heads. Since they were sculpted on a stick, they are easy to mount on a wire body. The kind that were sculpted around a core of some other material are also fairly easy to mount, since the neck wire can probably be stuck right into the core material. On the other hand, if you used a stuffed cloth body (which would give you a reasonable facsimile of an antique doll), you would have to glue the head to the cloth of the body.

Fig. 16-2 A papier mâché head (shown here relatively large) has a rough look before it's sanded.

Papier Mâché Babydoll

To make the baby in Figure 16-1, you need papier mâché head and hands, a small wrapped wire body about 5 inches long and the following materials.

    9" x 17" of white cotton for slip
    ¼ yard of organdy for dress and bonnet
    40" strip of lace for trim

5″ strip of elastic for gathering the sleeves

9″ of white bias tape for binding the neckline and back seam

ASSEMBLY

    Cut all fabric parts after enlarging the pattern in Figure 16–3.

    Slip. Bind the neck and armhole edges of the slip by turning the edges under and stitching. Fold the slip along the shoulder line and sew the side seams. Hem the bottom and put the slip on the doll.

    Dress. Pleat both the front and back of the dress as indicated on the

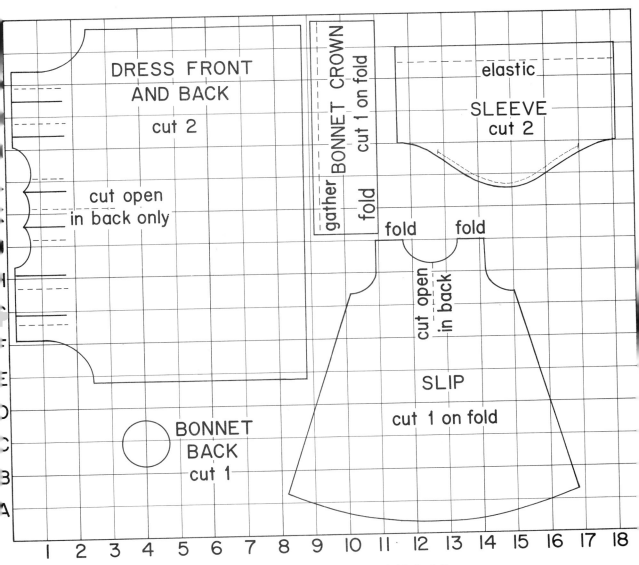

Fig. 16–3 Clothing pattern for papier mâché babydoll.

pattern: solid lines indicate the outside fold of each pleat, while the dotted lines indicate the inside fold. Place the front and back halves of the dress together and sew the shoulder seams. Next, bind the complete neck edge and the edges of the slit down the back with white bias tape.

Run a gathering thread around the top of each sleeve and hem the bottom of each sleeve. Stitch about 2½ inches of elastic inside each sleeve about a half inch from the end: stretch the elastic as you stitch, so that it is attached to the entire width of the sleeve. Finally, sew the sleeve seams and side seams, hem the bottom edge of the dress and sew the strips of lace around the bottom of the dress and the sleeve ends.

Bonnet. Fold the rectangular bonnet piece in half along the fold line with right sides together, then sew the short sides together. Turn the bonnet piece right side out and run a gathering thread completely along the unsewn edge. Next, sew the two circular bonnet pieces together, one on top of the other. Pull up the gathers in the large bonnet piece so that the gathered edge fits around the edge of the circular bonnet pieces. Sew the two sections of the bonnet together, the gathered edge going completely around the circular pieces.

Sew a strip of lace along the front edge of the bonnet and extend the lace a half inch or so on each side, so that, when the bonnet is placed on the doll's head, the lace strips will extend under the doll's chin. Place the bonnet on the doll and fasten the ends of the two lace strips together under the doll's chin with a couple of loops of white thread.

Accessories. The only accessories I used on this one are the rattle and a baby bracelet, both swiped from commercial dolls.

Chapter 17

Molded Felt Folks

I'm not sure that dolls with molded felt heads are really "folk art." After all, molded felt has been used by some of the most famous professional doll makers in the world, such as Di E. Scavinna of Italy, and Peggy Nesbit and Nora Wellings, both of England. Still, I like to make them occasionally, and I figure that anything I can make myself is folk art of a sort. Compared to the professional ones, mine are certainly folksy enough.

Working with Felt

The only part of the doll that is molded felt is the head. The rest of the body is usually very tightly stuffed felt, though other types of bodies could be used. I've always had the best luck with felt, though, so I'll stick with it. A couple recent ones of mine are shown in Figure 17–1.

Fig. 17–1 A baby in bunting and the Denim Dolly are made entirely of felt with molded faces.

MOLDING FACES

To be completely original in this, you would have to sculpt an original face in clay and use that as a mold for the felt. That's not for me, however, so I cheat a bit by using the heads of other dolls or the heads of metal or plastic statuettes.

If you're going to use a doll head to mold the felt, use one that has molded hair and painted eyes. This gives you a nice, clean surface to work with. Real hair and other fastened-on features just get in the way during the molding and they could well be damaged beyond repair by the gook the felt has been dipped in.

Once you've found a plastic doll with a face you like, pull the head off. If you're careful enough, you may be able to replace the head when you're finished with it and no one will know the difference. Actually, though it is clumsier to accomplish, you could leave the head on the body during the molding.

Cut a round piece of felt about 4 inches wider than the face of the doll. That is, if the doll face is 2 inches wide, cut a circle of felt 6 inches in diameter. Next, wet the circle of felt with tap water that is hot, but not hot enough to burn your hands. This will shrink the felt rather quickly, but don't worry about that; you will be stretching it again. And if you didn't shrink it to begin with, the later stretching might tear it.

Put the wet felt over the doll's face. Pull the felt taut in all directions and then push it into all the features, until the fabric is completely form fitting and the doll's features show clearly through the felt. Fasten the felt in place by stretching a wide rubber band tightly around the whole head—under the chin and over the top of the head. At this point, you should have something that looks roughly like Figure 17–2.

Now allow the felt to dry for a day or two, but check back every half hour or so during the first few hours to be sure the felt doesn't pull loose from any of the features. If necessary, poke the eyeholes, etc., back in every so often. If you wish, you can spray a little starch over the whole thing at any time during the drying. This will give the face more stiffness when it is dried. Spray sparingly, though; more than one quick spray and the felt will probably become shiny.

When the felt feels dry to the touch, *cut the rubber band off* (removing the rubber band without cutting it could crush the felt if the felt slips away from the head before you get the rubber band clear). Remove the head from behind the mask. Pull the felt off carefully, but don't worry if it seems to stick a bit. It won't cling too tightly and the felt will work back into shape in the next step.

Make a half-and-half mixture of white glue and water; use your finger to smear this mixture quite heavily all over the inside of the felt mask. Make sure all the depressions and irregularities are liberally covered. Allow this to dry a few hours and the felt should become quite stiff, about as firm as one of the plastic Halloween faces you buy in variety stores. If it still feels a bit soft, smear some more glue-and-water mixture inside the mask and let it dry again. When the felt is suitably dry and stiff, cut off the excess felt (everything beyond where the rubber band was).

Fig. 17–2 The wet, molded felt mask formed around the doll's head.

MAKING BODY PARTS

To make the body for the doll in the bib overalls in Figure 17–1, you will need 12″ x 18″ of felt, some string and four buttons. The doll is about 12 inches high, including the head.

Cut the body pieces according to the pattern in Figure 17–3 after enlarging it onto 1-inch graph paper.

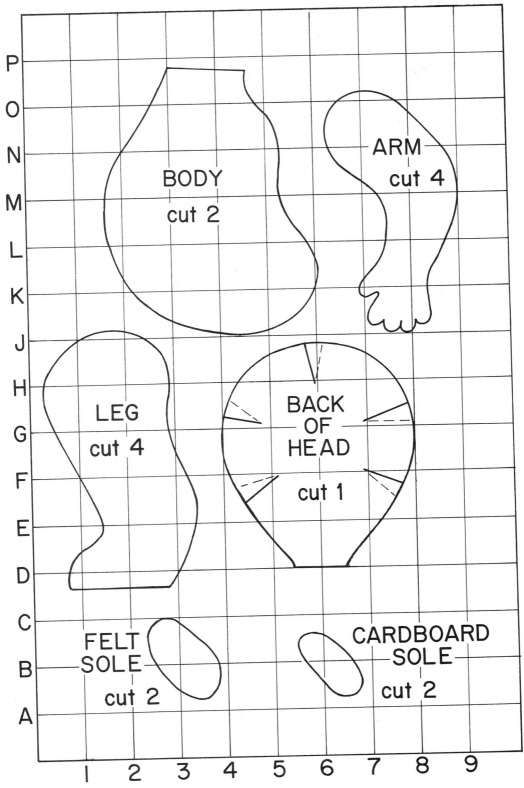

Fig. 17–3 Body parts pattern for the Denim Dolly.

For felt dolls much less than 20 inches high, I sew the body pieces together using an overcast stitch. For really large dolls, you can make a standard inside-out seam using a sewing machine or, if you don't have one, a running stitch or a backstitch.

Start with the torso. Sew the two halves together, but leave the neck opening for stuffing. Similarly, for the legs, sew entirely around except for the bottom of the foot. Leave the sole open for stuffing.

The arms are a little more complicated. First, stitch from the wrist, down around the ends of the fingers and back to the other side of the wrist. Next, stuff the hands tightly, then run a few short backstitches between all the fingers. Pull the stitches down tightly enough to actually give the impression of separate fingers. Once the hand is suitably stuffed and stitched, sew the arm halves together the rest of the way around the edges, except for a stuffing opening at the shoulder end.

To stuff the torso, arms and legs, use a dowel of some kind to stuff everything very firmly. If there are any small corners, make sure those are filled up first. If necessary, push tiny bits of stuffing into the corners with the point of a knitting needle. Once the corners and crevices are filled, go on to the rest.

When the arms are completely stuffed, sew up the shoulder end tightly. When the legs are completely stuffed, place the sole of the foot, together with the reinforcing piece of sole-shaped cardboard, over the foot opening and stitch the felt in place with short overcast stitches. When the body is stuffed, leave the neck open until you're ready to attach the head.

FINISHING HEADS

Since you probably haven't used a doll face that was precisely the same size as the one I used for molding, the head pattern can give you only the rough shape that you want. You will have to do some cutting and adjusting to make it match the face part of your doll. Start by cutting a piece of felt that is at least large enough and lay it over the front of the mask to get an idea of the exact size. Press it down around the edges of the mask and pin the necessary darts in.

Once the back head piece is shaped and the darts are pinned in, remove it from around the mask and cut slits for the darts. Stitch the darts, then cut off as much of the excess felt as possible.

Now, place the back of the head in position against the mask and, if it fits, put a few pins in to hold it in place. The back part should overlap the edges of the mask slightly, just enough to give you something to stitch through, perhaps an eighth of an inch. Sew the two halves together with an overcast stitch. Don't worry if the seam isn't too neat or invisible. For one thing, it's very hard to stitch through hardened felt neatly. For another, the stitches will be mostly covered by the hair you add later. To give yourself the best chance, of course, use thread that matches the felt as closely as possible.

Once the two halves of the head are suitably attached to each other, stuff the head. Again, be sure to get all the small crevices completely filled.

ASSEMBLING HEAD AND BODY

To attach the head to the body, start by positioning the head the way you want it (i.e., looking straight ahead, to one side, etc.) and pinning it to the body. Then stitch by hand all the way around the neck, using a ladder stitch. As you stitch, continue to poke more stuffing into the neck so that, when you finish, the neck will be stuffed firmly and the head won't wobble.

The arms and legs are attached as shown in Figure 17–4. Use a long darning needle (the kind used for upholstery work), strong string or twine and some flat buttons $\frac{1}{4}$" to $\frac{1}{2}$" in diameter. Just run the needle through one button, through the arm or leg, through the body, through the other arm or leg, through the second button. Next, run the needle back through everything again in the opposite direction, using different holes in the buttons. Once the string is all the way through in both directions, pull it up tight, drawing the limbs firmly in against the body, then tie the two ends of the string together. Just be careful not to pull the strings in so tightly that any parts of the doll get squashed. Make several knots just to be sure it won't come apart and cut the ends of the string.

PAINTING FACES

Painting the face is the trickiest part of the whole operation. If you like, you can copy the face that was on the doll you used for a mold, but I prefer to make up a different one. In either case, start by lightly drawing in the features with a soft lead pencil. Using these as a guide, you can paint the final features on.

I've found that artist's oil paint works nicely on felt. Other kinds, such as acrylics and enamels, tend to run and smear. If you plan to mix different colors to get a particular shade, be sure to do the mixing before putting any of it on the doll. Unlike nuts or other hard-surfaced dolls, the felt will absorb the paint before you have a chance to do any blending.

Oil paints, as I've said before, take a long time to dry, so just let the newly painted doll sit around in some out-of-the-way place for a week or so before you handle it or even look at it any more. I say this because, if you have the doll someplace where you can see it fairly often, the temptation to poke at the paint to see if it's dry may be overwhelming. If you do and the paint isn't dry yet, you will have a doll with a permanent fingerprint on its face. That is, the

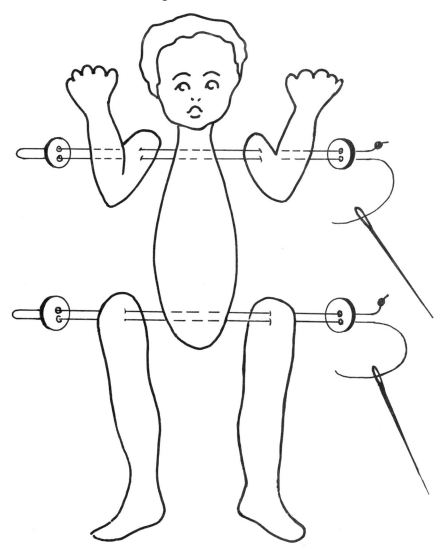

Fig. 17–4   Assembling the five parts of the stuffed felt body
using thread and buttons.

paint will smear, just as it will on the hard-surfaced dolls, but you will not be able to clean the paint off and start over. The felt will have absorbed too much for that. The best you can do is put another, thicker layer of paint on over the smeared layer.

After the face is dry, put on a yarn wig or paint on hair in whatever style you prefer. I like yarn wigs for a couple of reasons. For one, they just look better than paint. The paint is too stark or severe for a felt doll. Yarn, on the other hand, has a texture that matches the felt. Also, the yarn covers up the seam between the two halves of the head much better than paint would.

Denim Dolly

Materials

To make the clothes for the doll with the bib overalls shown in Figure 17–1, you will need the following materials.

9″ x 17″ of denim for the overalls
a scrap of contrasting color, for the patch
11″ square of cotton print fabric for the shirt

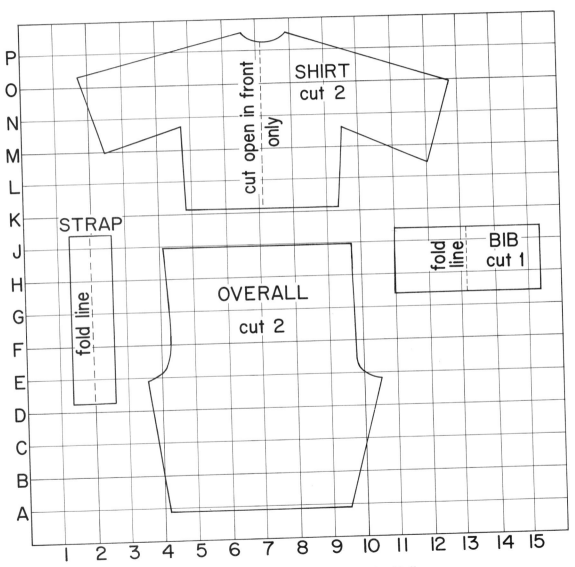

Fig. 17–5 Clothing pattern for the Denim Dolly.

8″ of bias tape for binding the neck and front of the shirt
4″ elastic strip, for gathering the overalls

ASSEMBLY

Enlarge the pattern in Figure 17–5 onto 1-inch square graph paper and cut out all fabric parts.

Shirt. Place the front and back of the shirt together and sew the shoulder seams. Bind the neck opening and the right side (as seen from the front) of the front opening in the shirt. Hem the other side of the front opening and the sleeve edges. Next, sew the sleeve and side seams, then hem completely around the bottom. Finally, sew on two or three snaps that can be used to fasten the shirt front together after it's on the doll. Add a couple of buttons for show, not for function. Put the shirt on the doll and fasten the snaps.

Overalls. Place the right and left halves of the overalls together and sew the front and back center seams. Hem the leg bottoms and then sew the inseam. Fold the bib piece in half along the fold line with the two right sides together, then sew the two side edges together. Turn the bib right side out.

Fold the strap pieces in half along the fold line, the two right sides together, and sew along the long edges. To turn the straps right side out, now, will take a little patience. This is one case where a forceps or strong tweezers would come in handy. (If you don't want to go to all this trouble, fold and sew the straps right side out.)

To gather in the waist of the overalls, sew a 4-inch strip of elastic inside the back of the overalls, starting about an inch to one side of the bib edge and running completely around the back to within an inch of the other bib edge.

Sew buckles or snaps on the straps and the top of the bib. For my buckles, I used the remnants of an old garter belt which I had stashed away in one of my odds and ends boxes for a few years. Because of the snaps on the shirt and the elastic and strap hooks on the overalls, the clothes for this doll can be taken off and put on easily.

Chapter 18

Selling
and
Displaying
Dolls

In the last few years, there's been a great demand for almost any items that are handmade or even look as if they were handmade. If you're at all like me, any doll you make will have a decidedly handmade look about it, so if you have the time and inclination, you will probably find a ready market for all you can make. At the very least, most of your friends will want a few. Most gift shops, particularly the kind that cater to tourists, will be happy to handle your salable items. In today's newspaper, for example, I saw three different ads placed by gift shops, all looking for handmade items to sell on consignment. I live in a fairly small city that is not overrun with tourists, so I imagine these ads are fairly common in most areas.

Selling

CONSIGNMENT

The best way to get a shop to handle your dolls is to make up several as a sample of what you can do. If you want to specialize in one kind of doll—such as appleheads—make up a variety of these, all dressed differently, and take them to the nearest gift shop. If the proprietor likes your work, he will usually take a batch on consignment. This means that he will display and sell them in his shop in exchange for a percentage of the sale price. Figure out how much you want to get, add the commission on top of that, and you're in business. You won't get rich at this sort of thing, but it can at least give you a little extra spending money now and then. And it won't cost you anything if they don't sell.

CRAFT SHOW EXHIBITS

If you have a great many dolls to sell and really want to go into business for yourself, you can eliminate the commission by setting up a booth at a local craftshow or flea market, if there are any in your locale. Make this a one-day-at-a-time arrangement, though, since it is hard to predict how long it will take to sell the dolls you have. You will have to pay rent for the space, of course, but that will be only a few dollars. The thing to keep in mind is that, unless you have a cooperative friend or relative you can dragoon into watching the table for you occasionally, you will have to stay right there, glued to your dolls so to speak, the whole time the market is open. However, you can work on a doll while sitting there. This always seems to attract people and will give you another one to sell!

If you want to do it the really easy way, run a classified ad in your local paper. That way you can just stay home and wait for the calls. You can be working on other projects while you wait.

Word of mouth can be the best advertising. If you find that you can make one type of doll particularly well, then specialize in that one and offer a doll to a collector or two. Don't offer to give it away, though; offer it at your standard price. If it's different and/or well made, you will soon have all the orders you can handle. Doll collecting right now is one of the most popular hobbies in the country, so there are plenty of collectors looking for a bargain or for something unique.

PRICING DOLLS

Don't price yourself out of the market. Handmade dolls rarely turn into a full time business, so keep this in mind when putting a price on your dolls. Unless you are either extremely fast or extremely talented—or both—you will find it almost impossible to charge enough to get yourself even the current minimum wage for the number of hours it takes you to make the dolls. People just can't afford to pay that much for a doll, as a rule. However, if you keep your doll making as a fun-to-do thing and are able to sell them for at least three times the cost of the materials (if any), or one to two dollars an hour for your labor, you will come up with a pretty fair market value. This will give you enough money for more supplies and a bit extra for yourself. As for me, I get a great deal of satisfaction out of buying a birthday or Christmas present for my husband with the money I earn from the dolls.

In any event, you will probably have to consider doll making strictly a spare time activity and just enjoy what you're doing. The pleasure you take in creating them will show through in the quality of the finished product.

Displaying

AT HOME

If you want to make dolls to keep for yourself—and what's wrong with collecting your own dolls?—you will need to consider the proper place to set them. Cardboard boxes full of dolls aren't too esthetically pleasing.

There are dozens of places around the average house to put them: bookshelves, cabinet tops, window ledges, coffee tables, speaker enclosures, the ledges over doors—any place, in fact, that you can find an unoccupied surface. You can even hang them in midair like mobiles, especially if you make a shrunken head or two (Ch. 14). Dolls with wrapped wire bodies, of course, can be positioned any way you want, so you can very often get by without a stand. Just put them in sitting position and place them on the edge of something, their feet dangling over the edge.

For many of the dolls, though, you will need some kind of support; most of them look better when they're standing, anyway. The clothes don't look as wrinkled, for one thing. A few of the small ones, such as clothespin or smaller nut dolls, can be made to be totally self-supporting with a sufficiently wide, stiff skirt. Or, if the skirt is wide but not stiff, put a small cardboard tube over the doll's legs. For larger, more top-heavy dolls of the same kind, put the legs into an ordinary water glass and wedge them in place by filling the glass with wadded up paper or cloth.

For some of the applehead and nut dolls, a small chair is often appropriate, especially a rocking chair. (I like chairs because my husband is very handy at making them.) If you want any of your unskirted wire bodied dolls to stand alone, glue the feet to a small square of sanded wood large enough to keep the doll upright.

The gourd heads and other dolls with heavy heads will require a stand of some sort. One such stand is shown in Figure 18–1. To make this one, use a piece of dowel about the same length as the doll's body. Drill a hole for the dowel in a block of wood, then drill a small hole through the dowel near one end. Glue the undrilled end of the dowel into the hole in the block. To stand the doll up, simply wrap a fine wire around the doll under its arms, put both ends of the wire through the hole in the dowel and wrap the ends around the

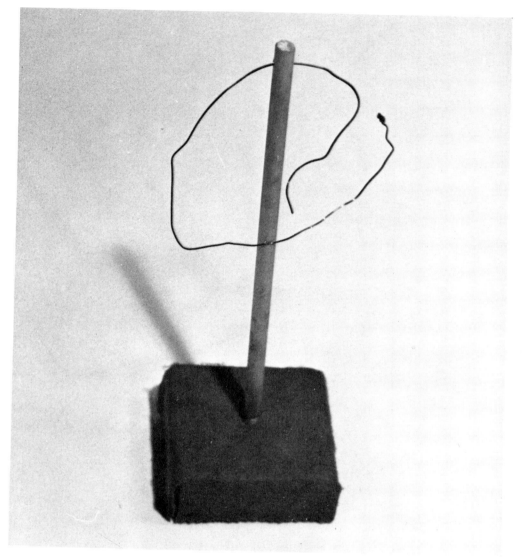

Fig. 18-1   A stand you can easily make at home for holding dolls safely upright.

dowel a couple of times. This type of stand will hold all but the very heaviest dolls. If you cover the wood block with felt or some other colorful material or paint it an attractive color, it won't look out of place at all.

FOR SALE

To display dolls for sale, set them up in action groups. Never just line them up as if they were waiting for the class photographer. (Never mind the fact that most of the pictures in the book look that way. Do as I say, not as I do.) Arrange them so they appear to be doing something, anything—reading miniature newspapers, talking, having parties, shoveling snow, squaring off for a brawl. It doesn't really matter, just so they're doing something: this adds a great deal to the appeal of the dolls. They look individual, the way they're supposed to, not as if they were run off an assembly line, which is how they look if they're simply lined up in a row. Also, such displays attract the customer's attention. He may stop just to see what the dolls are doing, especially if you can come up with some imaginative activities, and he may stay long enough to buy one. Even if he doesn't buy, chances are good that he'll strike up a conversation about the dolls and that's always fun, too.

And, as I keep repeating, that's what I'm in this for: fun. If it ever stops being fun, that's when I stop making dolls. But the way things are going lately, it doesn't look like I'll stop for quite a few years yet.

Index

Gini Rogowski

Born April 8, 1931, I have been married for 25 years, have four sons aged 24 to 15, and a 10-year-old daughter who loves—but fortunately does not own any—horses. We live in beautiful suburban Oak Creek, Wisconsin, downwind from a three-stack powerplant. At various times our household has included two lambs, a half dozen Easter chicks that grew all too rapidly into roosters, a calf and assorted conventional pets. At present, we are reduced to our overly friendly Boxer, Trina, a hamster named Priscilla, and an undefined pup named Barney that a friend rescued from a blizzardy New York wayside last winter.

My husband Bob has the most useful hobby in the family: he makes shelves by the dozen for me. I guess he figures that's easier than shoveling his way through piles of my dolls whenever he wants to get from one room to another. At other times, when it's all too much for him, he and the boys head for nearby Lake Michigan with their scuba-diving gear. Since I never learned to swim, that type of diving is out for me, but I did try sky diving once. Not for long, though: one successful jump was enough to prove to myself that 1) I could do it, and 2) I didn't want to do it any more. My more everyday hobbies and activities include knitting, needlepoint, crocheting, home canning, and, of course, making, repairing and collecting dolls.